Helen Keller

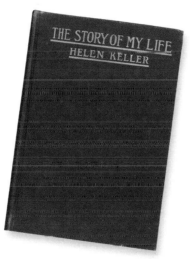

Helen Keller

Leslie Garrett

DK Publishing, Inc.

LONDON, NEW YORK, MELBOURNE,
MUNICH, AND DELHI

Designed for DK Publishing
by Mark Johnson Davies

Editor : Elizabeth Hester
Series Editor : Beth Sutinis
Editorial Assistant : Madeline Farbman
Art Director : Dirk Kaufman
Publisher : Chuck Lang
Creative Director : Tina Vaughan
Photo Research : Tracy Armstead
Production : Chris Avgherinos
DTP Designer : Milos Orlovic

First American Edition, 2004

04 05 06 07 08 10 9 8 7 6 5 4 3 2 1
Published in the United States
by DK Publishing, Inc.
375 Hudson St., New York, New York 10014

A catalog record for this book is available
from the Library of Congress.

ISBN: 0-7566-0339-0 (PB)
ISBN: 0-7566-0488-5 (HC)

Color reproduction by GRB Editrice s.r.l., Italy
Printed and bound in China by
South China Printing Co., Ltd.

Photography credits:
Cover photos Border images, from left to right:
Library of Congress, Prints & Photographs Division: a;
©Time Life Pictures/Getty Images: b;
© Mark L Stephenson/Corbis: c; © Bettmann/Corbis: d;
©Wray Dillard: e; Courtesy Perkins School for the Blind,
Watertown, Massachusetts: f; ©AP Wide World: g;
Courtesy American Federation of the Blind: h.
Front jacket, main image: ©Bradley Smith/Corbis.
Spine: ©Time Life Pictures/Getty Images.
Back jacket, main image: ©Bettmann/Corbis.

Discover more at
www.dk.com

Contents

chapter 1

A Remarkable Life

Helen Keller ran her fingers down the pages of her Braille Bible, taking in every word. Her days ended the same way they began, by reading her Bible. Finishing the last page, she closed her book and placed it on the table beside her bed. She closed her sightless eyes and welcomed sleep.

In 1960, Helen Keller was 80 years old and still fairly active—often entertaining friends and going for the

Helen Keller traveled to many countries, changing attitudes toward the blind and deaf.

walks she loved to take with her dog. But she was growing tired. More and more, she preferred to stay in with her books. Helen loved books. Both blind and deaf since the age of 19 months, Helen knew she was lucky to be able to read and write.

Though some blind and deaf-blind people of Helen's era lived their lives shut away, Helen had achieved great things. She had not only mastered the everyday tasks that those of us who see and hear take for granted—such as getting herself dressed and eating with a knife and fork— she'd learned to speak, read in four languages, write and type on a typewriter and a Braillewriter, and been educated at one of the best universities in the world.

Helen Keller remains a symbol of the human spirit's ability to overcome limitations.

She had also fought hard for her beliefs, many of which were daring for the time, including the right of women to vote. She had lectured tirelessly about fighting poverty as a way to prevent some causes of blindness. She had attended rallies supporting unions

In Braille, letters, numbers, punctuation, and speech sounds are represented by 63 different combinations of six raised dots.

and written influential articles about racial equality, child labor, and unfair work practices. Helen had met kings, emperors, and presidents. She was as comfortable with the world's wealthiest people as she was with the poorest. And now, after a lifetime of effort and optimism, she was one of the best-known and most respected women in the world.

Through it all, Helen had one wish: She wanted the world to accept her as no different from someone who could see and hear. She had worked hard to show the world not only that she could do anything, but that other disabled people could, too. She knew she had achieved her purpose. She also knew she couldn't have done it alone.

None of it would have been possible if not for that day almost

"While they were saying among themselves it cannot be done, it was done."

Helen Keller

eight decades earlier when Teacher arrived at the Keller's home. Annie Sullivan, whom Helen called Teacher her whole life, had been the first to reach six-year-old Helen in her dark, silent world, and show her all that life could hold. Helen and Annie were well matched—both had bright minds that were always seeking out the next challenge. It was once said that the world considered Helen Keller a miracle. But to Helen, the miracle was Annie.

Helen frequently took walks, during which she "talked" to herself with her fingers.

chapter 2

A Horrible Fever

Kate Keller was frantic. Her daughter's fever would not let up. Kate held her daughter, Helen, through the long days and nights, trying to soothe the little girl. Helen could hardly sleep, and she tossed and turned, hot and hurting.

The doctor could offer little help—or hope. Helen was only one and a half years old. He didn't expect her to live through this "brain fever." In the late 1800s, there were so many diseases a parent had to worry about—scarlet fever, meningitis, smallpox, tuberculosis. Many of them were deadly.

After several days, Helen's fever broke at last. Kate hugged her daughter close, grateful that the little girl had survived. No one, not even the doctors, knew yet what the fever had done to Helen.

Later that day, Kate went to Helen,

Ivy Green was the Kellers' family home. It was built in 1820.

lying in her little bed. Sunlight streamed in the windows and shone right on Helen's face. Though the little girl's eyes were open, she didn't turn from the bright light. Curious, Kate waved her hands in front of Helen's face. Helen didn't blink. Kate took a lamp from a nearby table and shone the bright light directly into her daughter's eyes. Still nothing.

Childhood diseases

Measles and mumps killed children in the 1800s, but today are prevented with vaccines. Other deadly diseases, such as scarlet fever and meningitis, are now treated with antibiotics. Helen's illness was diagnosed by her doctor as "acute congestion of the stomach and brain" or "brain fever." It was most likely actually a case of scarlet fever or meningitis.

Terror welled up as the truth sunk in: little Helen was blind.

A few days later, Kate was with Helen when the dinner bell rang. Before she'd become ill, Helen, who loved to eat, had always stopped whatever she was doing at the sound of the bell and raced to the table, eager to get to the food. This day, however, Helen didn't even seem to notice.

Kate picked up a homemade rattle, a can filled with stones. She held it beside Helen's ear, then gave it a shake. Nothing. Kate shook it again, louder. Helen didn't move.

The fever had left Helen deaf, too. Kate simply sighed and held her daughter tight. She didn't know what challenges lay ahead—but it was clear that Helen's life would never be easy.

Over the next few years, the Kellers traveled from doctor to doctor with Helen. None of them could help. Helen,

MUTE/DUMB

People who are mute are unable to speak. In Helen's day, they were called dumb.

trapped in a dark, silent world, became more and more frustrated. She often had temper tantrums during which she would kick and scream like a wild animal.

In those days, many believed that a bad fever left its victim an "idiot." Because Helen's behavior was so wild and uncontrollable, some people, including some of Helen's relatives, thought the little girl belonged in an insane asylum.

The future for Helen looked hopeless. But the Kellers, particularly Helen's mother, refused to give up.

Helen depended on her mother and often trailed behind her around the house, holding on to Kate's skirts. Helen also adored her father and liked to imitate him reading the newspaper, mimicking the

Helen's father, Captain Arthur Keller, was a newspaper editor. Her mother, Kate Keller, took care of the house and children.

way she felt his hands holding it up and even putting on his glasses.

Helen grew to know the other members of the household: her half brothers, James and William; her Aunt Ev, who lived with the Kellers and whom Helen loved; and the Kellers' servants.

Because she could neither hear people speak nor see their mouths move, Helen did not learn language as a seeing, hearing child would. Instead, she used her own simple signs. A shake of the head meant no; a nod meant yes. For bread, she would imitate the cutting and buttering of slices. For ice cream, she would shiver. If she wanted her mother, she would stroke her own cheek. Before long, Helen had developed more than 60 signs.

Helen's mother, especially, came to understand Helen and Helen to understand her. But even at such a young age, Helen realized she was different. She noticed that other people talked with their mouths. Helen tried to talk also, moving her lips frantically. But when no one understood her "speech," Helen became more frustrated.

Trapped in her dark and silent world, Helen more and more often gave in to howling fits of anger.

chapter 3

Asking for Help

Though she was unable to see or hear, five-year-old Helen was good at getting into mischief. Her playmate was Martha Washington, the child of the Kellers' cook. Martha understood Helen's signs and usually gave in to whatever Helen wanted.

The two friends spent a lot of time in the kitchen, helping to knead dough, make ice cream, and feed the hens and turkeys that flocked to the kitchen steps in search of food.

One day, left alone, the girls sat on the porch, cutting out paper dolls. When they tired of cutting paper, they put their scissors to work on other objects—their shoelaces, the nearby honeysuckle leaves. Then Helen seized one of Martha's bunches of black hair, which were tied with strings all over her head. *Snip* went the scissors. Then Martha took the scissors and cut off one of Helen's

Helen later referred to her angry self as "phantom" and the time before Annie Sullivan came to her as a "no-world."

long curls. It was then that Helen's mother appeared and ended the game before both children were completely bald.

One of Helen's pranks was to lock people in rooms. One day she locked her mother in the pantry, a room off the kitchen where food was stored. Helen could feel her mother pounding on the door while the little girl sat, laughing with delight, on the porch steps. Three hours passed before Helen's mother was finally found and released.

The Kellers endured Helen's childhood pranks to a point—until her behavior became a danger to Mildred, her new baby sister.

Before Helen's time, Laura Bridgman had been famous for her own achievements. But she lacked Helen's outgoing personality and charm.

One day, Helen discovered little Mildred sleeping in one of Helen's most prized possessions: her favorite doll's cradle. Furious, Helen toppled the cradle. Mildred wasn't hurt, but everyone knew she could have been. They also knew the time had come to find someone—anyone—who could help Helen.

Then Kate Keller came across a story about a deaf-blind woman named Laura Bridgman. In his book *American Notes*, Charles Dickens wrote about visiting the Perkins Institution, a school for the blind in Boston, Massachusetts. There he had met Laura. Like Helen, Laura had become blind and deaf as a child. She had been taught by Dr. Samuel Gridley

Howe, a respected teacher of the blind and those with special needs. Dickens wrote that Laura had learned to communicate through the manual alphabet, a system devised to communicate with the deaf. In the system, each letter of the alphabet was shown by a different hand position. For Laura, who also couldn't see, Dr. Howe had adapted the manual alphabet so she could "feel" the hand signs. Laura had learned to communicate…and by doing so, she had escaped her own dark, isolated world. Her success was

Alexander Graham Bell

Alexander Graham Bell was born on March 3, 1847, in Edinburgh, Scotland. His father and grandfather were speech experts, and his mother was deaf. Even as a child, Bell was fascinated by sound, and he became interested in the education of the deaf. He invented a type of microphone and, in 1876, the telephone. Helen and Dr. Bell became lifelong friends, and she credited him with bringing her "from isolation to friendship, knowledge, [and] love."

remarkable. *If it had worked for Laura Bridgman,* thought Kate Keller, *then why not Helen?*

Feeling more hopeful, the Kellers took Helen with them to meet an eye doctor in Baltimore. Though he admitted that he could do nothing to restore Helen's sight, he declared that she

clearly had a clever mind and could be educated. He suggested that the Kellers get in touch with Alexander Graham Bell. Dr. Bell was an expert on teaching speech to the deaf. Surely he could give the Kellers advice on schools and teachers for Helen.

"I did not dream that that interview would be the door through which I should pass from darkness into light."

Helen Keller

Helen loved meeting Dr. Bell. She happily climbed up on his lap and played with his watch. He was kind and tender with Helen, and the two became fast friends. Dr. Bell easily understood many of the signs she had created for herself to communicate.

Dr. Bell advised Helen's father to ask Michael Anagnos, director of the Perkins Institution, to send a teacher for Helen. Captain Keller made the request, and, in the summer of 1886, a letter came. A teacher had been found, the Kellers read. That teacher was Anne Mansfield Sullivan.

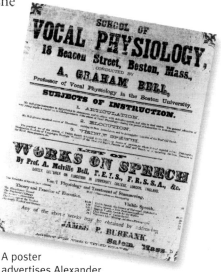

A poster advertises Alexander Graham Bell's lectures on speech and sound.

17

4

Annie

A nne Sullivan, like Helen, had a childhood marked by loss and anger, though in very different ways. Annie, as she became known, lived with her father, Thomas, and mother, Alice, in Feeding Hills, Massachusetts. Though money was scarce, they always had food on the table and shoes on their feet. Alice was kind and warm; Thomas was funny and full of stories. Annie loved to hear her father's tales. After dinner, she would climb into his lap and listen happily.

But when Annie was three years old, her left eye began to itch. She had an infection. The more she rubbed, the more damaged her eyes became.

Her parents had no money for a doctor, so they waited, hoping that Annie's eyes would heal on their own. Two years passed. Annie wasn't any better, so her parents finally took her to a doctor. The problem was trachoma. The doctor knew the Sullivans couldn't pay for the treatments Annie needed. He gave them some medicine to put in Annie's eyes, but it didn't help.

Then Annie's mother developed a sore throat and cough that wouldn't go away. It was tuberculosis, a leading cause of death in the United States in the 1800s. Alice was also expecting a child. The baby,

TRACHOMA

Trachoma is an eye infection caused by bacteria. It was a major cause of blindness in the 1800s.

named Jimmie, was
born with a disfigured
hip, a result of Alice's
tuberculosis. But things
would grow even worse
for the Sullivans.

As Alice grew pale and weak, Thomas Sullivan became
distant and angry. He often drank. Another baby, Mary, was
born. Annie watched it all with sore, tired eyes.

Finally, Alice died. The children stayed with their father
at first, but when his drinking got worse, they were sent to
live with an aunt and uncle. After a while, the
relatives didn't want the older
children—one with sick eyes and
an awful temper, the other with a
lame hip. Mary, the youngest—
and healthiest—could stay. On
February 22, 1876, when Annie
was 10 years old, she and five-
year-old Jimmie were sent to the
poorhouse—the place where
people went when they had
nothing.

Annie and Jimmie were the
only children at the Tewksbury
Almshouse, except for the
newborns in the orphans ward.

Annie Sullivan had a temper as
quick and wild as Helen's. She
earned the nickname Miss
Spitfire as a teenager.

19

The two stuck together, surrounded by the prostitutes and sick old ladies in the women's ward. The newborn babies usually died. The food was full of bugs, and the rooms had rats. But Annie and Jimmie had each other, and they clung together fiercely.

As weeks passed, Jimmie's hip grew worse. Then he couldn't get out of bed at all. Soon, Annie's beloved brother died. Annie had no one.

Days turned to months, then weeks, then years. Annie didn't dare dream of getting out of Tewksbury. Her eyes were growing worse—she was almost completely blind. It seemed hopeless. Then an old resident at Tewksbury told her about a special school. It was called Perkins Institution for the Blind. Annie hung on to the hope that there was somewhere in the world for her.

Some laughed at Annie's dream of going to Perkins. But Annie had made some friends at Tewksbury, and she turned to them for advice. Annie's friends told her about a group of important people who were going to visit. One of them, Frank B. Sanborn, was connected with Perkins. When the visitors arrived, Annie asked whomever she could find for Frank B. Sanborn. "Please send me to school," she pleaded to the strangers.

Finally, someone stopped and asked Annie what was wrong with her. Annie said she couldn't see, but she wanted to go to school. *How long have you been here?* she was asked

"I don't know," replied Annie. After a few more questions, the people left.

Annie was crushed that they had left without offering to help her. She went to bed and wept. She was sure that her last hope had vanished. But a few days later, Annie was told to pack her things. She was going to Perkins.

Perkins wasn't at all like Annie had imagined. She was in a class with students who had been attending school regularly. Annie hadn't. She was 14, and she couldn't read or write. She couldn't add or subtract.

So Perkins put her in kindergarten. Annie felt foolish sitting in a class with six-year-olds. The older students teased her, and Annie's quick temper got her into plenty of trouble. She was homesick for Tewksbury. It may have been awful, but to Annie, it had been home.

But Annie's quick mind served her well. She learned to read raised print with her fingertips. She also learned to read Braille. She was catching up to the students her age. But Annie often lost her temper.

A poorhouse offered shelter and food for those with nowhere else to go. The conditions were often dismal.

with the other students. One day she went too far and became furious with a teacher. Annie stormed out of the classroom, shouting that she'd never return.

The director of the school, Michael Anagnos, didn't know what to do with this wild girl. He knew he should send her back to Tewksbury, but he couldn't quite bring himself to do it.

Then another teacher came to Annie's rescue. She was sure that if Annie could just learn to control her temper, she'd be a brilliant student. The teacher was right. She not only taught Annie her studies, she gave her manners. Slowly Annie began to mimic her, speaking softly and kindly to others. She learned not to get angry when the other girls teased her. Over the next six years, Annie found other friends and grew to love Perkins. She became one of the school's best students. She helped with younger students. She even graduated as class valedictorian and was invited by her house mother to spend the summer on Cape Cod.

But Annie spent her summer worrying. How was she going to support herself? She had an education, but

Perkins Institution for the Blind was the first school for blind children in the United States.

what was she going to do with it? Then, Annie received a letter from Mr. Anagnos. He enclosed the letter he'd received from the Kellers, seeking a teacher, and asked Annie to consider the job. Annie wasn't sure. Yes, she needed a job, but was she up to the task of teaching another Laura Bridgman?

Annie had come to know Laura at Perkins, where the older woman still lived. Annie felt sorry for the older lady, sewing alone in her room, and would visit and try to communicate with her.

Annie decided to find out more. She spent months reading Dr. Howe's files about teaching Laura. She knew it would be hard to teach a blind, deaf, and mute child—the more she read, the more she realized just how hard.

But by early 1887, Annie felt as ready as she'd ever be to take on the task of educating Helen Keller.

The Perkins Institution for the Blind

The founders of the Perkins Institution set out to create a school that helped blind people to learn rather than making them charity cases. The Perkins School opened its doors in 1832, and quickly gained an excellent reputation for its teaching methods and its supportive, nurturing environment. Today, Perkins continues to teach blind and deaf-blind students, as well as those with other disabilities.

chapter 5

A Stranger Arrives

Helen knew that March 3, 1887, was no ordinary day. All around her, she could feel the household preparing for something…but what? The house had been cleaned and the guest room aired out; wonderful smells were coming from the kitchen. Then Helen's mother put on her gloves and hat, which Helen knew meant that she was going out.

Helen stood on the front porch steps, expectant. She could feel the warm sun on her face. She took in the scent of the nearby honeysuckle and fingered the leaves and blossoms. She felt anxious but had no way to ask what was happening. She would have to wait.

Kate Keller and her stepson James had been going to the Tuscumbia train station for two days, meeting every

The Tuscumbia, Alabama, train station was located about a mile from the Kellers' home.

train that arrived in their small southern town. No Annie Sullivan. Kate was getting nervous. She didn't even want to imagine what they'd do if Annie never came.

On March 3, they waited, yet again, for the final train to arrive at the station. Only a few people got off. One of them was Annie Sullivan.

Annie was not in a good mood. A ticket agent had sold her tickets for a train that stopped at almost every

Annie Sullivan was 20 years old when she took on the task of educating Helen Keller.

town between Boston and Tuscumbia, instead of the express she'd wanted. The trip had taken three days instead of one. She was hot and tired, her eyes were sore, and her dress wrinkled. Nonetheless, she stood tall on the platform, smoothing her skirts and straightening her glasses, which were dark to protect her sensitive eyes from the sunlight. Then she looked around for the Kellers.

James came to greet her, leading her over to the carriage. Annie looked for Helen. She was disappointed when she heard that Helen was waiting at the house. But Annie figured if she'd waited this long, she could wait a little longer.

Annie climbed in beside Kate Keller. The two women liked each other right away, and Annie felt confident that she had a friend in Helen's mother. She didn't know yet how much she'd need one.

The carriage came to a stop in front of a pretty white house with green shutters. A carefully tended garden surrounded the home. But Annie barely noticed. She was looking for Helen.

Captain Keller greeted the carriage and its occupants with his hand outstretched. Annie took it but instead of offering a greeting, she asked, "Where's Helen?"

Captain Keller's gaze turned to the front porch. Annie followed his eyes and saw a little girl standing in the shadows, her body rigid. Helen pulled at the leaves of a vine, ripping them off. She knew the carriage had arrived, but she was unsure what was happening. So she stood, ready, and waiting.

Ivy Green is located on 640 acres. It was built by Helen's grandparents and named for the ivy that covered its exterior.

Annie caught her breath. She was shocked at Helen's appearance— the six-year-old's hair hung in tangles, and her dress and stockings were filthy and torn. Her brown shoes were tied with white string.

Annie made her way toward Helen.

Helen felt footsteps approaching. Though she could

hear nothing, she had learned to "feel" sound through vibrations in the ground or air. Thinking it was her mother, Helen stretched out her arms for a hug.

Annie took the little girl in her arms. But Helen pulled back. Surprised, Annie tightened her grip. Helen twisted out of her arms, struggling to get free. She growled and kicked like a wild animal until the others told Annie to let go.

Kate Keller explained that since losing her sight and hearing, Helen didn't like being held, except by her mother.

"You were brought here to teach a wild animal," said James, who was quickly shushed by his father. But Annie had to wonder. Helen seemed almost more wild animal than little girl.

Helen, meanwhile, stood off to the side. Curious, she returned to Annie. She reached out her hand to touch the stranger. Annie stood still and let Helen feel her way to Annie's face. She felt Annie's round glasses, nose, mouth, and dusty dress. Annie laughed. Helen was a bold little girl—not the least bit afraid.

Annie realized that Helen's hands had been her eyes. They had taught her everything she knew. And now it was up to Annie to open up the world to her through those hands. Those hands, Annie knew, would set Helen's mind free.

chapter **6**

First Glimpse of Success

Annie knew the kind of discrimination blind people faced. The deaf-blind, like Helen, were even worse off. They were thought impossible to educate or even to handle. Like Helen, many deaf-blind children grew frustrated and threw temper tantrums. Some people, including some of Helen's relatives, believed they should be put away in an asylum. But Annie was determined not to let that happen to Helen.

Some dolls from Helen's era would have had heads made of fragile porcelain, like the doll pictured here.

On Annie's first morning at Ivy Green, Helen came to her room. Helen walked around, feeling the stranger's things. Her hands discovered Annie's suitcase and opened it up. Inside, Helen found a doll. It was a present for Helen from the students at Perkins. Laura Bridgman had sewn a beautiful outfit for it to wear. Helen loved dolls. Delighted, she hugged the doll close.

Well, thought Annie, this is as good a time as any to start. She took Helen's hand. D-O-L-L. She

carefully spelled the letters into Helen's palm using the manual alphabet. Then Annie took Helen's hand and patted the doll's head, to bring her attention back to the doll. Over and over again Annie repeated the actions—first spelling the word into Helen's hand, then patting the doll's head.

Helen stood rigid as she focused on these odd flutterings in her hand.

Kate Keller poked her head into the room. Curious, she asked Annie to explain what she was doing. Annie showed how she'd spell the letters—

Finger Spelling

Many deaf or hearing-impaired people talk with their fingers, using a system of manual signs or finger spelling. The basic system was created by Spanish monks to communicate without breaking their vow of silence. The language was modified in the 1700s by Abbé Charles Michel de l'Epée in France, then brought to America by Laurent Clerc, a teacher of the deaf.

D-O-L-L—into Helen's hand, then move her hand to the doll. What she hoped, Annie explained, was that Helen would learn to connect the name of the object with the object itself.

Soon Helen began to shape the letters herself. What a bright child, realized Annie. But when she saw the look of hope on Kate Keller's face, Annie quickly explained that Helen was simply copying what Annie had done. But, she added, one day she would connect the two things—the object and its name. That was the key. Once Helen understood language, learning would become, perhaps not easy, but possible.

Annie turned back to Helen. She lifted the doll from Helen's arms. If Helen could spell doll on her fingers, then Annie would return the doll. But Helen had another idea. Furious that the doll had been taken from her, Helen's voice erupted in something like a growl. Her fingers curled into fists and she launched herself full strength at Annie. Annie was ready. She grabbed Helen's arms and held them tight.

But Annie would not give the doll back. Not until Helen learned to obey.

With Annie holding tight, Helen finally stopped struggling. Annie loosened her grip, and Helen sprang free and raced from the room.

But curiosity always brought her back. Though at first

Annie lived with the Kellers at Ivy Green. At first she stayed in her own room, but later shared a room with Helen.

Helen was fascinated with Annie's finger play, she would sometimes tire of it. Annie learned to let Helen set the pace, and when she'd had enough, Annie was content to drop the lesson...for the time being. Instead, they would go for a walk or play a game. But at the first opportunity, Annie would again seize Helen's hand and begin spelling into it. M-U-G, she would spell. H-A-T. Then S-I-T, S-T-A-N-D, W-A-L-K.

But Annie was realizing that before she could reach Helen's mind, she had to teach Helen to control her quick temper and strong will. Helen was determined to get her own way. Annie was just as determined not to let her.

One day, while Annie was in her room, Helen crept outside the door. Silently feeling for the keyhole, Helen found the key still in the lock. In a flash, Helen turned the key in the lock, yanked it from the keyhole and disappeared, stopping only to slide the key beneath a piece of furniture.

In her room, Annie heard the click of the key. She raced to the door and pulled. It wouldn't budge. She was locked in. She yelled for help.

Kate Keller came running. It didn't take long to figure out what had happened. It was Helen's favorite prank.

Nobody had another key, and Helen was nowhere to be found. Captain Keller brought out a ladder and placed it at Annie's window. Then he climbed up, retrieved Annie, and carefully brought her down.

Annie was furious. But she had to admit one thing. Helen had a quick—though sometimes devious—mind.

chapter 7

Taming the Wild Child

Helen quickly became interested in the stranger at her house, but Annie could do little to improve her bad behavior. Helen was a tiny tyrant, using brute force to get whatever she wanted. Her parents usually gave in rather than upsetting Helen further. Annie would not, and teacher and student often clashed.

After Annie had been with the Kellers a few days, she decided she'd had enough of Helen's temper and rudeness.

That morning, Annie sat down with the Kellers for breakfast. As usual, Helen picked out her favorite food from her own plate with her fingers, then stuffed her mouth with it. Annie was shocked—and disgusted—by Helen's poor table manners. Then Annie watched as Helen climbed down from her chair and wandered around the table. When she smelled something she liked on another person's plate, she reached out and helped herself to it.

She came around to Annie's spot. She sniffed. Sausage, her nose told her. Yum! Helen's hand darted out to grab it. Annie's hand came down hard on Helen's. The little girl tried to pull it free, but Annie held tight.

Helen howled and managed to yank her hand away. Then she tried again. Again, her hand was pinned beneath Annie's. Helen was furious. The Kellers pleaded with Annie to give Helen what she wanted.

Annie refused, suggesting that the family leave if they found her discipline upsetting. Annie was not going to let Helen get away with this behavior. She was going to teach her student self-control. The family walked out, leaving Annie and Helen alone.

Helen tried again. But Annie wouldn't budge. After throwing a tantrum, Helen went from chair to chair, figuring out who else besides Annie was in the room. No one was there. She raced to the door and pulled with all her might. It wouldn't budge. She was locked in with the stranger.

Helen went to her chair and began to finish her own breakfast with her fingers. Annie forced a spoon into her hand. Helen threw the spoon to the floor. Annie pushed Helen down on the floor and made

The Kellers ate at a formal dining room table—but Helen had terrible manners.

her pick up her spoon and finish eating with it. After several refusals, Helen finally gave in, sat down, and finished her breakfast using her spoon.

But the battle wasn't over yet. Now Annie wanted Helen to fold her napkin. Instead, Helen threw it on the floor. Again, Annie forced Helen down on the floor to pick it up and fold it. Helen began a tantrum, kicking and screaming. Another hour passed. Finally, Helen gave in to Annie's will, picked up her napkin and folded it as Annie showed her. Annie unlocked the door and released Helen into the warm sunshine.

Annie was exhausted. She dragged herself up to her room, where she lay on her bed and wept. She may have won this battle, but she knew there were plenty more to come.

The only answer, she knew, was to get Helen away. Without her parents giving in to her all the time, Helen would have no choice but to begin obeying Annie. And only when Helen learned self-control could learning really begin.

Annie approached the Kellers about her plan. She was surprised when they agreed. But they insisted that Helen stay close by.

In Helen's bedroom, her favorite doll, Nancy, had a cradle at the foot of the bed.

Helen was born in a small cottage on the Keller property and had lived there as a very young child. Now she returned with Annie to begin her education.

Captain Keller suggested Helen and Annie move into the small, unused cottage on the property, where Helen had been born.

Captain and Mrs. Keller asked that they be allowed to see her every day. Annie agreed, but with one condition. Helen must not know they were watching.

Plans were made to ensure that Helen didn't realize how close she was to her home. The furniture in the small cottage was rearranged so that it would be unfamiliar to Helen. Then, Helen was taken on a long, roundabout carriage ride so that she would think she was being taken far away. Finally, she was led to the cottage—with just Annie and a young servant.

Things didn't improve between Annie and Helen. At least not immediately.

> *"Obedience is the gateway through which knowledge and love enter the mind of a child."*
>
> Annie Sullivan

That first day, Helen played with her beloved dolls. She ate well, then got undressed for bed. But when she felt Annie climb into bed with her, she leaped out and refused to get back in.

Annie insisted and found herself battling Helen again. For two hours, she tried to get Helen back into bed. She finally succeeded, though Annie noted later, "I never saw such strength and endurance in a child." Helen finally fell asleep, tired and troubled, as close to the edge of the bed—and as far away from Annie—as possible.

The next morning, Helen was homesick. The little girl kept going to the door. Then she would touch her cheek, which was Helen's sign for her mother. She wanted nothing to do with Annie and eventually sat down to play alone with her dolls for much of the day.

But Helen's sadness didn't change Annie's mind. She was sure that, in time, Helen would settle down and learn to trust her.

It didn't happen right away. The days dragged on, and Annie and Helen continued to fight—about getting dressed, buttoning shoes, brushing hair. The Kellers watched. One day in particular, they were so dismayed by a fight Annie and Helen had over getting dressed that Captain Keller said he was ready to send Annie packing.

He didn't, though. And shortly afterward Helen seemed to change. Annie wrote in a letter that "The wild creature of two weeks ago has been transformed into a gentle child…. It now remains my pleasant task to mold and direct the beautiful soul that is beginning to stir."

What had finally worked to "transform" Helen? Annie had a subtle but effective tool. Though Helen didn't yet understand the connection between words and objects, her interest and curiosity were stirred by Annie's almost constant spelling into her hand. Helen even tried spelling into her dog Belle's paw. To Helen it was just a game. But when she didn't behave, Annie refused to "talk" to her by refusing to spell into her hand. To Helen, this was torture. She was back in her solitary world— dark, silent, alone. Helen quickly learned that if she wanted company, she had to behave.

Helen was learning. Soon would come the event that people have called "the miracle."

Helen had a lifelong love of dogs and always had at least one or two. She even tried finger spelling into their paws.

chapter 8

T-E-A-C-H-E-R

Annie was puzzled. Helen was learning new words daily, but it still didn't seem as if she was making the connection between word and object. Two words, in particular, were a struggle for Helen: "mug" and "milk." Annie knew that Helen was confusing those two words with the verb "drink." Whenever Helen spelled "mug" or "milk" into Annie's hand, she would mimic the act of drinking. Annie was getting frustrated. They had spent a month working together, but Helen still hadn't figured out that things and actions were different. She still hadn't attached meaning to words.

Helen was frustrated, too. She picked up a new doll and threw it to the ground. She could feel the fragments scatter around her feet, so she knew it had broken. But she didn't feel badly for what she'd done.

Annie sighed, sweeping the broken

pieces toward the fireplace hearth.

Suddenly, she had an idea. Helen loved playing in the cool ground around the water pump. It was beautiful that morning of April 5, 1887, so Annie took Helen's hand and led her outside to the water pump. She showed Helen how to hold the mug under the water and Annie pumped it into the mug and over Helen's hand.

The pump at Helen's home (above) was central to one of the most important moments in Helen's life, dramatized (below) in the movie *The Miracle Worker*.

W-A-T-E-R, she spelled into Helen's palm, first slowly then faster. In a second, Helen dropped the mug and Annie saw that Helen's face seemed to brighten. Quickly, Annie did it again. W-A-T-E-R. W-A-T-E-R.

In an instant, Helen understood. Everything had a name. Each word belonged to one of the objects that Helen had known all her life, she realized, and now she could finally describe them. This cold, wet something was W-A-T-E-R.

Helen rushed around touching everything so Annie could tell her what it was. Falling to the ground, she asked its name. D-I-R-T, spelled Annie. Then P-U-M-P. Then H-E-L-E-N. And finally, T-E-A-C-H-E-R.

In the Schoolhouse

Most children in Helen's town would have attended a one-room schoolhouse. One teacher would likely have taught all grades, from first through eighth. Children were seated by grade and studied reading, math, spelling, history, and geography. Students took notes with chalk on small chalkboards. There were few books or supplies.

When they went back inside, Helen remembered the doll she had broken. Suddenly, she realized what she'd done. This had been a D-O-L-L, her doll. She felt her way to the fireplace hearth and, with tears in her eyes, tried to put the doll back together. When she couldn't, she felt something she'd never felt before—regret.

Still, nothing could erase the happiness both Annie and Helen felt as they flitted around the house. Helen demanded to know what everything was, and Annie was delighted to tell her. Before the day was through, Helen had learned 30 new words. When Helen went to bed that evening, she was happier than she'd ever been. She described it later in her autobiography, *The Story of My Life*, "For the first time [I] longed for a new day to come."

The days tumbled by into summer. Annie and Helen spent their days outside, eagerly exploring the world around them. Annie discovered that Helen was happiest when she was moving, so many of the lessons took place outdoors where Helen could run and touch and play. It was by the banks of the Tennessee River that Annie taught Helen about nature: how the sun and rain make trees and crops grow, how animals and birds find food and shelter. Helen finally felt like a part of the world around her. By summer's end, she'd learned 625 words.

But words were only the beginning for Helen. Just like hearing children, Helen learned words first and then had to learn to put those words together to communicate a thought or an idea. Helen was hungry for words, and Annie spelled constantly.

Then Annie decided that Helen was ready for the next step. Annie pulled out a big card with the 26 letters of the alphabet written in raised lettering. This was one of the ways that the blind learned to read. She placed Helen's hand on the letter A. Then she spelled the letter into Helen's palm. Helen was confused. She understood what was happening in one hand. But what was this shape

Annie used finger spelling to communicate with Helen, often spelling into Helen's hand for hours at a time.

beneath her fingers of the other hand? Annie didn't explain. She simply moved Helen's fingers to the next letter: B. Then C. Suddenly Helen understood. By the end of the day, Helen had learned all the letters of the alphabet. She knew these letters were put together to make words, though she wouldn't learn to spell with them until later.

Annie understood that Helen's learning had to be accompanied by life experience. One day, she decided to take Helen to see the circus. Helen was thrilled to help feed the elephants and to play with the monkeys, who tried to steal flowers from her hat. She felt the length of a giraffe's neck, the huge paw of a bear. She even followed the circus performers around the ring. Helen was becoming a part of the world around her, and it felt wonderful to her.

Annie was as amazed as anyone by how quickly Helen was

Letter cards allow a blind person to feel the shape of a written letter. Helen used cards like these to learn all 26 letters of the alphabet in a single day.

learning. Her seven-year-old student knew as many words as a hearing, seeing seven-year-old.

But just knowing the words wasn't enough. Teacher, as Helen called Annie, realized that if Helen was ever to truly understand language, she had to learn it as much as possible in the same way a hearing child learns it. A hearing child listens to the talk around him all day long, long before he knows what the words mean. Slowly the child picks up phrases and words, almost by absorbing them. Annie decided to treat Helen as if she were a two-year-old child, who

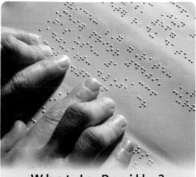

What Is Braille?

Braille was created in 1825 by 16-year-old Louis Braille. "Night reading," in which raised dots in a pattern spell out messages, had been created for the French army. Based on this idea, Braille developed his system for the blind. To read each letter, a person uses the most sensitive part of the index finger—the area between the tip and the first joint. The other fingers serve as a guide. A skilled Braille reader can read up to 150 words a minute—about half as fast as a sighted reader.

understood words, but had not yet learned to talk. She "talked" into Helen's hands almost constantly, from morning to night. She told Helen about anything and everything, sometimes using new words without offering the meanings, sometimes using "idioms," or expressions that are part of our

> **"*Something tells me that I'm going to succeed beyond my wildest dreams.*"**
>
> Annie Sullivan

language. It was very different from the way Laura Bridgman had been taught and different from the methods used to teach deaf children Helen's age. But it began to work. Years later, when Helen explained how she had learned language, she credited Teacher with creating the method and noted, "Life tumbled upon [me] full of meaning."

Annie felt inspired by Helen's success. She wrote about it in a letter to a friend. "Something tells me," she wrote, "that I'm going to succeed beyond my wildest dreams."

Annie was already fulfilling the Kellers' dreams. When Christmas arrived in 1887, the Kellers truly had reason to celebrate.

Helen had been invited by the schoolchildren of Tuscumbia to share in their Christmas Eve. It was a thrill to the Kellers; Helen's previous tantrums meant that she'd rarely been included in events outside her home. Now, Helen was asked not only to join, but also to help give out the gifts that were piled beneath the Christmas tree. When one little girl didn't receive a gift, Helen even offered one of her own.

Helen was too excited to fall asleep that night. She lay awake for a long time, hoping for some sign that Santa Claus had arrived before finally drifting off. The next morning, Helen woke long before the sun rose. She couldn't wait to find out what Santa Claus had brought her. She woke the household and then ran downstairs. There were presents in her stocking and beneath the tree—as Helen described it, she could "hardly walk without stumbling on a bit of Christmas all wrapped up in tissue paper." But her favorite gift was from Teacher—a canary named Little Tim that was tame enough to be held in Helen's hand.

The house was a far different place than it had been the previous Christmas. Kate Keller, who had learned finger spelling to communicate with Helen, thanked Annie with tears in her eyes. "I thank God every day of my life for sending you to us, but I never realized until this morning what a blessing you have been to us," she said. This Helen was not the same Helen, with her tantrums and tricks. She had undergone an almost unimaginable change. This Helen had Teacher. Annie was opening up a world to her, as if she was being wakened from a long, dark sleep.

For Annie, who found tiny, rural Tuscumbia very dull, her first year with Helen was difficult. She thought of leaving, but her growing love for Helen kept her from acting on it.

chapter 9

Opening Her Mind

Helen was a wonderful student. She was eager for each lesson to begin and easily learned the words Annie was teaching her. One morning, Helen brought Annie some violets she had found in the garden. Annie took Helen's hand and spelled, "I love Helen," into it. Helen asked what "love" was. Annie tried to

Stringing glass beads helped Helen learn to imitate patterns as she felt the difference between pieces.

explain by pointing to Helen's heart. But Helen could only attach meaning to something she could touch. Frustrated, the two of them gave up…for the moment.

A few days later, Helen was stringing beads in a pattern. She puzzled over an arrangement that she knew was wrong, but she was unsure how to make it right. Annie touched Helen's forehead and spelled "think" in Helen's hand. Helen realized that what was happening in her head was thinking. For the first time, she understood that some things can't be touched or felt or even sensed. They are abstract ideas or thoughts.

ABSTRACT

A word or concept is abstract if it has no simple or clear connection with a physical object.

She wondered again about "love" and asked Annie. Love, her teacher explained, was like the clouds that give rain and help flowers grow. She pointed out that Helen couldn't touch the clouds, but she could feel the rain and enjoy the flowers. Love, she continued, was similar. You couldn't touch love, but you could feel how sweet it made the days and feel the joy that love creates. As Helen later wrote in her autobiography, "The beautiful truth burst upon my mind—I felt that there were invisible lines stretched between my spirit and the spirit of others."

Learning to read Braille at the Perkins Institution allowed Helen to read books on her own.

Now that Helen was beginning to master language (though the process would continue for several years), the next step was to teach her to read. Annie gave Helen pieces of cardboard with words spelled on them in raised print. Helen quickly learned that each word stood for an object, action, or

Helen loved books because, she said, "No barrier of the senses shuts me out from...my book-friends. They talk to me without embarrassment or awkwardness."

description. Then Helen would put together a sentence using the words, but also creating a scene using the objects themselves. For example, Helen might lay her doll on the bed, and place the word "doll" on her. Then she'd put the words "is," "on," "the," and "bed" beside the doll.

One day, Helen thought she'd have some fun with Annie. It had been a long time since she'd locked Annie in her room, but she still liked pranks. Helen pinned the word "girl" on her own dress. Then she placed the words "is", "in," "the" and "wardrobe" so that Annie would be led to where Helen was hiding.

Nature played a key role in Helen's education. Many lessons were conducted outside, where Helen could explore through touch.

Helen was so excited, she could barely wait. She stood in the wardrobe, trying hard to be patient, waiting for the vibrations on the floor that would tell her Annie was coming. Helen could usually tell who was coming and going based on the feel of the vibrations on the floor.

After what seemed like a long time, she felt Annie coming…closer…closer. Finally Annie opened the wardrobe to discover "girl" inside. She was delighted…but not as much

> *"I know that Helen has remarkable powers and I believe that I shall be able to develop and mold them."*
>
> Annie Sullivan

as Helen, who was very proud of herself. The two played at this game for hours. Everything in the room became arranged in sentences.

But Helen learned just as much from the real world as she did from raised alphabet sheets and word cards. Since Annie had first come to Helen's home, she had made sure that Helen "saw" as much as possible through touch. One day, she brought Helen a warm egg. Hold it gently, Annie told Helen. *Why?* wondered Helen. Eggs were for eating. But while she tried to figure out what was different about this one, she felt it move. Then, to her surprise, she felt the shell crack and out popped a damp baby bird.

Helen gained an appreciation for how things grow from feeling a lily change over a few days from pointed buds to silky petals. She learned about frogs by plunging her hands into a bowl full of tadpoles. She loved the feel of them slipping and sliding between her fingers. Helen held crickets in her hand to feel their distinctive chirp. She felt the low wind rustle the cornstalks.

Helen learned about birds hatching by holding a warm egg in her hand while a tiny bird pecked its way out.

Nothing held Annie and Helen back. Together they rode horses and sailed boats on the Tennessee River. They even went tobogganing in the winter.

Annie was determined that Helen learn from the things that interested and excited her. Helen's favorite walk was to an old wharf on the river. Out of the pebbles, water, and clay there, Annie and Helen created mountains, islands, lakes, buried cities, dams, and valleys. To Helen, it was fun; to Annie, it was geography. As Helen later said, she "learned from life itself."

There were days, though, that Helen felt as bored as any child trapped in a classroom. Arithmetic, she admitted, she did not like. And though Annie tried to teach it by using beads on string and straws, it remained something Helen wished she could avoid.

Language was Helen's passion, and Annie couldn't spell fast enough or long enough to satisfy Helen's hunger for words. She begged for stories, and Annie was happy to oblige, though Annie's own eyes often grew tired from reading. She insisted that Helen know only good literature, and so the two read the classics, such as *The Iliad* and *The Odyssey*, as well as Shakespeare and the Bible.

But only a few months after Annie's arrival, the

Helen's Journal

With Annie's encouragement, Helen began keeping a daily journal about her life. It was a practice she kept up for most of her life. In 1936, following the death of Annie Sullivan, Helen's journal was published.

intensive learning was taking a toll on both of them. Helen was finger spelling constantly—even to her dog and baby sister. When her parents saw that she would rather talk with her hands than use them to eat, they called in the doctor. He diagnosed her as suffering from "an overactive mind." Annie herself had frequent headaches and trouble sleeping.

Helen wrote by placing paper over a grooved writing board. She moved her pencil within each square to make a letter.

Annie tried to slow down, for herself and Helen. But if she refused to spell into Helen's hand, the little girl simply talked nonstop into her own hand. However, the doctor's order to rest helped both of them recover before they resumed their studies.

In her first year with Annie, Helen learned to spell 900 words and write letters. Shortly before her eighth birthday, Annie had Helen start a journal. She wrote in pencil on paper fitted over a grooved writing board using block letters. The entries generally revealed Helen's day-to-day life. It was about to become much more exciting.

chapter 10

Ready for the Outside World

Annie had been writing faithfully to Michael Anagnos at the Perkins Institution since the day she had arrived in Tuscumbia, more than a year earlier. Anagnos was thrilled at the progress Annie was making with Helen and often wrote about it in the Perkins newsletter. Though Annie was happy to be given credit for her teaching skill, it angered her that Anagnos referred to Helen as a "phenomenon" and exaggerated her skills. Annie felt that the real Helen should be impressive enough—a bright, kind, happy eight-year-old girl who was achieving great things.

Still, Annie was glad when Anagnos invited Helen and her to visit Perkins in May 1888. Annie was getting restless in Tuscumbia, and she thought that Helen was ready to experience the outside world. Also, Perkins offered resources that the Kellers simply didn't have—raised-print books, Braille books, and more. So Annie, Kate Keller, and Helen packed their bags and boarded the train north.

> **PHENOMENON**
> An unusual and remarkable person or thing is called a phenomenon.

The trio stopped in Washington, D.C., where they visited with Dr. Alexander Graham Bell, who had become a very good friend to Helen and Annie. They were also invited to the White House to meet President Grover Cleveland.

By the end of the month, they had arrived in Boston. Helen quickly made friends with the blind children at Perkins. "What joy," she wrote later, "to talk with other children in my own language!" In no time at all, Helen felt at home at Perkins.

Helen's hands-on education continued. Annie taught Helen about United States history with trips to Bunker Hill and Plymouth Rock.

In June, Helen was invited to participate in Perkins's graduation

Alexander Graham Bell remained an inspiration to Helen. She dedicated her first book to him.

Cape Cod is a popular tourist destination on the coast of Massachusetts.

exercises. She was seated beside the famous Laura Bridgman. But the crowd had arrived to see Helen. She stood and read a poem through Annie, and a newspaper reported that the audience was "moved to tears."

When Perkins closed for summer vacation, Helen, her mother, and Annie went to Cape Cod, where they spent the summer with Annie's former Perkins house mother. Helen had a wonderful time. Curious about the ocean, she waded right in. Suddenly, she was swept upside down by a wave, but Annie pulled her to safety. Rather than feeling frightened, Helen was indignant. "Who put salt in the water?" she demanded. She developed a love of the sea that would last the rest of her life.

A few months later, Annie, Kate, and Helen returned to Tuscumbia, where Helen's studies resumed. But Annie's eyes were bothering her more and more. As a result, the lessons were often shortened or interrupted. Annie decided to have surgery the following summer in Boston.

In fall 1889, Annie and Helen returned to Perkins, where Helen was welcomed as a guest of the school. This meant that, while Annie continued to be her main teacher, she had access to all of Perkins's resources, including its wonderful library and a taxidermy collection of animal and bird specimens to help her learn about the natural world.

Other Perkins teachers stepped in to help Annie, teaching Helen basket weaving, pottery, and music. Helen even learned to read and write in French in three months, stunning Anagnos, who could hardly believe that Helen had done in three months what might have taken a seeing, hearing child a year.

Mr. Anagnos continued to publish stories about Helen, each one more lavish in its praise than the one before. As a result, Helen was becoming known around the world.

In March 1890, while still at Perkins, Helen learned of a little girl in Norway—also deaf, blind, and mute—who had learned to speak with her mouth. Helen knew

Helen Learns Other Languages

Helen had a knack for learning language—any language, it seemed. After her incredible ability to master English, she went on to learn French, German, and Latin. She often scattered phrases in these other languages throughout her writing.

that others spoke with their mouths, and she wanted to do the same. She often put one hand on her throat and the other on her lips as she tried to make a noise. She decided that she, too, would learn to speak. Helen's decision was very daring. Annie tried to discourage Helen. But Helen would not be swayed. She insisted that Annie let her try.

Annie decided that if Helen was to learn how to speak, she would need the best teacher she could find. She took Helen to meet with Sarah Fuller, principal of the Horace Mann School for the Deaf, also in Boston, for advice. Fuller offered to teach the young girl herself.

Helen was thrilled. For as long as she could

Sarah Fuller, an expert on education, poses with her students at the Horace Mann School, where she was the principal.

Sarah Fuller

remember, she had wanted to learn to speak with her mouth. She remembered as a child that "Sometimes I stood between two persons who were conversing and touched their lips. I could not understand, and was vexed. I moved my lips and gesticulated frantically without result. This made me so angry at times that I kicked and screamed until I was exhausted." The only word Helen could utter was one she had learned as a baby, before losing her sight and hearing: *wah-wah* for water.

> ## The Science of Speech
>
> There are three main systems in the human body that help people create the sounds that make up speech. The first, the subglottal system, includes the lungs, diaphragm, and windpipe. This system's parts work together to create airflow. The larynx, or voice box, contains vocal cords, which cause the air to vibrate and take on sound. Finally, the supraglottal system shapes the sounds into words using the tongue, teeth, and lips. All of these parts were in perfect working order in Helen. The challenge was learning to put them to use.

Helen's thoughts often came faster than her hands could communicate them. Now, at the age of 10, Helen was getting her chance. On March 26, 1890, Helen and Sarah Fuller sat down to begin a task that many claimed was impossible.

Sarah Fuller began by placing Helen's hand on her face and in her mouth, lightly at first. This allowed Helen to feel the position of Fuller's tongue and lips when

she made a sound. Then Fuller shaped Helen's own mouth for making basic vowel sounds. She took Helen's hand and placed it on her throat so that the eager child

"Nothing that I have ever accomplished has cost me so dearly in time and effort."

Helen Keller

could feel the vibrations. For the next hour, with Helen gently touching Fuller's face, mouth, tongue, and throat, teacher and student intently focused on making the sounds of language. Helen's hands also probed her own mouth and neck, as she tried to copy what Fuller was doing. First she learned to form sounds. With time, she uttered her first sentence: "It is too warm." Though only Fuller and Annie Sullivan were able to understand what she was saying, they rejoiced just the same. It was a miraculous start.

Helen found the work exhausting but refused to give up. Fuller gave Helen only 11 lessons in all, but Helen practiced almost nonstop. She spoke to birds, to her toys, to her dog. When frustration mounted, she focused on the thrill she'd felt at uttering that first sentence. Then she'd force herself to carry on. She couldn't wait to show her family what she'd learned, especially her younger sister Mildred, whom Helen adored. She desperately wanted Mildred to be able to understand her. "I am not dumb now," Helen would repeat in delight, as she worked hard to improve her speech.

Annie had become as deeply determined as Helen. In

The Story of My Life, Helen wrote "I labored night and day before I could be understood even by my most intimate friends. I needed Miss Sullivan's assistance constantly in my efforts to articulate each sound clearly and to combine all sounds in a thousand ways."

Helen found speaking her thoughts far easier than the manual alphabet, and she quickly traded one form of communication for the other.

Finally, Helen was ready to go home. She and Annie boarded the train for Tuscumbia. Helen continued to speak nonstop to Annie, determined to improve until the last possible minute.

When the train pulled into the station, Helen's family was waiting on the platform—and Helen used her new skills to greet them all. Her mother pulled Helen close while Mildred danced in delight. Everyone was amazed, and Helen's heart filled with pride.

But Helen wasn't done amazing her family—or the world. Not yet.

Helen practiced speaking by feeling Annie's mouth, throat, and tongue as they formed a sound, and then trying to imitate Annie's speech.

chapter 11

"The Frost King"

Michael Anagnos continued to spread the word far and wide about Helen's accomplishments. Helen didn't know it, but over the years Anagnos had been publishing Helen's letters almost as soon as he received them. His connection to Helen Keller and her teacher was giving his school much-needed publicity and recognition. But Annie became increasingly angry with him. His reports on Helen's latest accomplishments were often exaggerated, yet newspapers picked the stories up, embellished them further, and relayed them as fact. Helen had learned to play the piano, they reported. She could read people's minds. The world was hungry for news and photos of this remarkable child, and Anagnos was happy to provide them.

Annie feared that Helen was being turned into an object of curiosity, rather than the real-life

Michael Anagnos was largely responsible for telling the world about Helen Keller. Because of his articles, Helen was world-famous by age 10.

little girl she was. Annie and Mr. Anagnos often exchanged emotional letters, with Annie criticizing him and Mr. Anagnos trying to defend himself. Their relationship was becoming strained.

Helen, however, either didn't know or didn't worry about such things. She considered Mr. Anagnos one of her very good friends. On November 4, 1891, Helen decided to send him a birthday gift. She wanted to give him a story she had written. She enclosed it with a letter telling him about her story, which she called "The Frost King." Anagnos loved Helen's story and published it along with her letter.

Not long after, however, he learned that Helen's story was quite similar to another story called "The Frost Fairies" by Margaret T. Canby. The Perkins director was very upset and embarassed that he had to print an apology. Helen was devastated. She had no memory of ever having been told the story, though it was later revealed that it had been spelled into her hand a few years earlier.

Though at first Michael Anagnos said he believed Helen had made an honest mistake, he later insisted she be charged with "plagiarism and deliberate falsehood." She was brought before him and eight other school officials. To Helen, it was torture. She was questioned before the committee for two hours. She left the room feeling dazed and deserted. That night, she wept uncontrollably and thought she couldn't survive the night. Though it was Anagnos who finally decided in Helen's favor that she was unaware that she was copying first two years. The house and outbuildings had to be repaired and repainted; and it was not until this present autumn—three years from the time she came home—that Catherine saw her way clear to pay off the mortgage and free the old place from its twenty years of bondage.

WHAT THE BLIND CAN DO.

BY HELEN KELLER.

> They meet with darkness in the daytime, and grope at noonday as in the night. —Job v. 14.

TO present to seeing people the truth about the blind is to describe a state of cruel deprivation, and at the same time tell a story of remarkable achievement. It is difficult for those who have not felt the terrors of blindness or known its triumphs to apprehend the position and requirements of the sightless. A great deal has been said and written about the blind; and yet persons well informed on other matters display a medieval ignorance about those who cannot see.

I have known intelligent people who believed that the sightless can tell colors by touch, and it is generally thought that they have one or more senses given them in place of the one they have lost, and that the senses which of right

I answer, "Help the adult blind to derive all the benefit possible from the education that has been so liberally given them. Help them to become efficient, useful citizens."

When blindness seizes a man in the midst of an active life, he has to face a greater misfortune than the child born blind or deprived of sight in the first years of life. Even if kindness and sympathy surround him, if his family is able to support him and care for him, he nevertheless feels himself a burden. He finds himself in the state of a helpless child, but with the heart and mind, the desires, instincts and ambitions of a man. Ignorant of what blind men can do and have done, he looks about him for work, but he looks in vain. Blindness bars every common way to usefulness and independence. Almost every industry, the very machin-

buildings equipped with the implements of learning, and does not render its benefits stronger and more serviceable citizens, by unwisdom the generosity that inspires and makes void its charity.

Blind graduates of these schools have said to me, in the bitterness of disappointed hopes and ambitions, "It would have been better to leave us in ignorance than to enlighten and cultivate our minds only to plunge us into a deeper darkness. What boots it that we have learned our youth in kindergartens, museums, libraries and music-rooms if we pass from those pleasant halls to sit with idle hands and eat the crust of discontent?" The time has come in strong and efficient measures should be taken in America to give the blind an opportunity to become self-supporting, or at least to earn a part of their support. In an age and country where the ability to work is regarded almost as a test of respectability, it is a disgrace that any man should be forced to sit in idleness.

WHAT DOCTOR HOWE DID.

THE blind as a rule are poor. The parents of most of the children in the institutions for the blind are working people. It is usually a bread-winner. It is hard for a young man to face his life

---

Helen's article was published in *The Youth's Companion* when she was 12 years old.

someone else's story, Helen felt completely betrayed by how she was treated. What upset Helen further still was her fear that she had no original ideas. She worried that everything in her mind had been put there by someone else—that she was incapable of forming her own thoughts and ideas. Even after she was known around the world for her accomplishments, the "Frost King" incident sometimes nagged at her mind and heart. In her autobiography, *The Story of My Life,* Helen wrote, "I have ever since been tortured by the fear that what I write is not my own."

Annie and Helen returned that spring to Tuscumbia. For a while, Helen stopped reading and even talking. She withdrew into her own

PLAGIARISM

Plagiarism is taking credit for the words or ideas of another.

> *"Only through experience of trial and suffering can the soul be strengthened, ambition inspired, and success achieved."*
>
> Helen Keller

world. The experience had shaken her to the core.

For some time after, Helen would hesitate when writing a letter or speaking with someone, then turn to Annie. Finger spelling, she would confide to Annie that she wasn't sure the idea was her own. Annie thought it might help restore Helen's confidence if Helen wrote about her own life in a children's magazine. She persuaded the 12-year-old to write her story in *The Youth's Companion*.

It worked. Though Helen began writing her story timidly and fearfully—she introduced her story with the words "Written wholly without help of any sort…"—she persevered. As Helen later wrote, she triumphed over the awful "Frost King" experience, "with a mind made clearer by trial and with a truer knowledge of life."

Michael Anagnos was so angry about "The Frost King" scandal that he called Helen "a living lie." Helen never forgave him for his treatment of her and Annie.

chapter 12

The Miracle Child

That year at Perkins had also given Helen a glimpse of her own future. She had learned about another deaf-blind boy named Tommy Stringer. Five-year-old Tommy lived in a poor-house and had no parents. The conditions were awful, and he couldn't go to school. Helen decided to help Tommy. She wrote to all her friends and even newspapers, asking for money to pay for Tommy to attend the Perkins Institution. Money poured in. It was enough to pay for Tommy's entire education. Helen was thrilled. She enjoyed helping Tommy and decided that she would spend her life trying to help others.

In the meantime, however, she still felt fragile about "The Frost King" incident. She often turned to Annie for reassurance that her ideas were hers alone. Slowly, her confidence came back. Helen

Helen (top left) wrote letters and articles asking people to contribute to Tommy Stringer's (bottom, right) tuition. She even denied herself treats to save money.

kept up her own writing, sending poems, stories, and letters to friends and family.

In 1893, Helen returned home with Annie. They continued with Helen's studies, but also ventured out often, exploring the world. While at Perkins, word spread about Helen's quick mind and amazing ability to learn. Mr. Anagnos had ensured that many people knew about Helen, and her fame continued to grow. She had been dubbed, "the Miracle Child," and now the public was hungry for news of the young girl.

On a sociable bicycle, two people could ride side by side.

Newspaper stories about her appeared frequently, and she was often photographed. In Maine, a shipbuilder named a ship after her. Helen was even invited to Washington for the inauguration of President Cleveland.

If Helen felt any pressure, she didn't show it. She enjoyed meeting the well-known people who contacted her. She and Dr. Bell remained good friends. She also became friends with many other wealthy and influential people of the time. Some of them even offered to support Annie and Helen financially. It was support that Helen and Annie sometimes had to rely

INAUGURATION
In an inauguration ceremony, an elected official takes an oath and takes office.

upon—Captain Keller was having financial problems and had stopped paying Annie's salary.

But most days, Helen was a fairly typical 13-year-old girl. She read her books, did her lessons, and had fun. Helen loved riding her horse, Black Beauty, and walking with her dogs. She also learned to ride a special bicycle called a "sociable" where the riders sit side by side. In bad weather, Helen would sometimes crochet or knit. And always, she would read. Helen loved books more than just about anything.

In the spring of 1893, Helen and Dr. Bell decided to surprise Annie with a trip to Niagara Falls, the huge waterfall between the United States and Canada. Even in 1893, Niagara Falls was a haven for tourists, who came to experience the thrill of 100,000 cubic feet of water rushing over the falls every second.

Helen could feel the power of Niagara Falls when she sat beside the rushing water. Annie, Helen, Alexander Graham Bell, and a friend posed for a picture there.

Helen Keller was no exception. Though she was unable to hear or see the magnificent falls, she was still impressed. She "felt" the water, she explained, and was awed by it, as are those who can see and hear the thunderous spectacle. With her hand against the window of her hotel room, she felt the water rushing past. Later, she traveled 120 feet down in an elevator to a deep gorge below the falls. Helen also crossed a suspension bridge 258 feet above the water to the Canadian side of the falls. And to help her enjoy the falls, Dr. Bell told her to hug a feather pillow against her, which magnified the feeling of the water's vibrations. Helen was thrilled!

When Helen expressed her delight with Niagara Falls, others were often taken by surprise. How could this girl appreciate what she could neither see nor hear? But Helen likened her interest in physical beauty to "love or religion or goodness," noting that you couldn't see or hear those things either, but they meant "everything."

That summer Annie and 13-year-old Helen again joined Dr. Alexander Graham Bell in Chicago for the World's Columbian

The Famous Helen Keller

The first biographies about Helen appeared before she was 10 years old. People were fascinated by her. Her celebrity status allowed her to travel all over the country and meet famous people. She learned that many people were eager to meet her. Captain Keller even talked about charging people to meet Helen and see her speak with her hands. But Annie fought hard against the idea. It never happened.

Exposition—the world's fair. The fair showcased great human achievements: inventions, art, history, food—plus carnival rides. The president of the fair gave Helen permission to touch the scientific, technological, and natural exhibits. It all came to life under her gentle touch. With Bell offering his fascinating explanations of what Helen was feeling, she explored a Viking ship, a diamond, and French bronze sculptures—her favorite. She also tried a new ride called the Ferris wheel, named after its creator, George Ferris, and nibbled a new snack that would later be named Cracker Jack.

Helen always took pride in her appearance and loved fancy dresses.

But to the other fairgoers, Helen was as fascinating as the exhibits themselves. She drew quite a crowd as she strolled from exhibit to exhibit with her equally celebrated companion, Dr. Bell. His invention, the telephone, was still very new in 1893. He had only opened the first long-distance telephone service the year before. Together they examined the telephones, phonographs, and other inventions as Dr. Bell explained how they operated.

Helen had a wonderful time. She later wrote that she felt as if she'd left a bit of childhood behind: "In the three weeks I spent at the fair I took a long leap from the little child's interest in fairy tales and toys to the appreciation of the real and the earnest in the workaday world."

Helen and Annie returned to Tuscumbia for a needed rest. But, as usual, they didn't stay in one place for long. In October, they went to stay with friends in Hulton, Pennsylvania, and Helen resumed her studies with a tutor assisted by Annie.

Helen was studying more subjects—and more difficult subjects—than ever before. In addition to improving her French, she began to study Latin with another tutor. Through him, Helen's love of books deepened, and she came to appreciate "an author, to recognize his style as I recognize the clasp of a friend's hand."

In the fall of 1894, Helen began attending a new school. One of Helen's wealthy friends, John Spaulding offered to pay for Helen's schooling; it had been decided that Helen should start at the Wright-Humason School for the Deaf in New York. It was a new school that aimed to teach the deaf to lipread and speak, something Dr. Bell strongly supported. He believed that the deaf should be integrated into society, and such skills could help.

LATIN

Many modern languages, including English, are largely based on Latin, the language that was spoken in ancient Rome.

Students at the Wright-Humason School for the Deaf studied lipreading and speech.

The school's founders, John Wright and Dr. Thomas Humason, promised Helen they could teach her to speak normally. It was just what Helen wanted. Though she practiced a lot, Helen's speech was still hard to understand. Helen was disappointed that she wasn't improving more quickly. She desperately wanted to be able to speak clearly. She was sure she could do more for others if only she could speak well enough give speeches and be easily understood.

So, together with Annie, Helen pinned her hopes on the Wright-Humason School. There she studied math, literature, and United States history. Helen also took singing lessons in the hopes of improving her voice for speaking.

But perhaps the most valuable skill Helen picked up at the school was the ability to lip read. Deaf people usually take in information by watching the way people's lips move when they form words. Helen, who couldn't see the speaker, had to learn a different way. Again, she relied on her hands. As she did when she was learning to speak, she placed her fingers on the speaker's throat to feel the vibrations, and on the speaker's lips and tongue to feel how they moved. At the same time, she felt how the air was going in and out of the speaker's mouth. Helen practiced constantly. At first, it was very difficult. But eventually, she learned—and it became her favorite way of understanding what others were saying to her, because it was so much faster than finger spelling.

At first, Helen was unsure about living in New York, but she quickly fell in love with Central Park, a large public park in

Helen and Annie were once described by Mark Twain as together "a complete and perfect whole."

the heart of the city. She and Annie rode horses there, and Helen liked to walk the wooded paths. In warm months, Helen and Annie sailed on the Hudson River. Helen loved the feel of gliding across the water. In the winter, Helen loved to toboggan. Soaring down a snowy hill, she felt a rush of freedom.

Annie and Helen met many influential and wealthy New Yorkers. While she genuinely liked many of them, Helen was unimpressed with their money. One day, she was invited to a reception at the Metropolitan Club, which, she noted in a letter to a friend, was often called the Millionaires' Club. "The building is magnificent, being built of white marble," she wrote "The

Harvard is one of the best colleges in the United States. In the 1800s, it was an all-male school, but both men and women attend today.

rooms are large and splendidly furnished; but I must confess, so much splendor is rather oppressive to me…I didn't envy the millionaires in the least all the happiness their gorgeous surroundings are supposed to bring them."

One day, Helen and Annie set out for New York's Lower East Side to see the slums where many of the new immigrants lived. Helen could smell the poverty—the dirt, the rot, the rats. It was an experience that moved her. Her already caring nature became even more sympathetic to those who had little or were afflicted by disease or disability. And though she counted many famous and influential people as lifetime friends, what she really wanted was to help those who were poor or weak and had little power to help themselves.

Another dream was also taking shape within Helen's mind. She had wanted to go to college since she was a little girl. Most of her friends either actively discouraged this desire or dismissed it as wishful thinking. But Helen remained determined. When she told Annie of her dream to go to Harvard University, her teacher thought it impossible. But Annie knew enough to not underestimate Helen. She simply said, "Not Harvard, Helen. That's a boys' school."

So Helen set her sights on Radcliffe College, which was associated with Harvard but created for women. She knew she would have to study very hard. But she was convinced it was possible.

However, there were a few hurdles Helen had to clear first.

chapter 13

Educating Helen

Helen Keller was still attending New York's Wright-Humason School for the Deaf in 1896 when she learned that her good friend and benefactor in Boston, John P. Spaulding, had died. Then, in August, she received word that her father had died suddenly. Helen was devastated. "My own dear loving father!" she wrote to a friend, "How shall I ever bear it!"

Helen did find some comfort in her growing spirituality. Alexander Graham Bell's secretary, John Hitz, had given her a book about the beliefs of a religious philosopher named Emanuel Swedenborg. Helen especially liked Swedenborg's idea of heaven. She grew to believe that "Death is no more than passing from

Commonwealth Avenue, one of Boston's main streets, features a grassy park and walkway.

one room into another." However she thought that for her there would be a difference because "In that other room, I shall be able to see."

Now, to help her deal with her father's death, Helen turned to the teachings she found so inspiring. She felt happier at the thought of her father in heaven, surrounded by angels.

She also turned her attention to plans for her education. Now that Helen had set her sights on Radcliffe, she needed to attend a school to prepare her. The Wright-Humason School hadn't

Emanuel Swedenborg

Emanuel Swedenborg was a religious philosopher in the 1700s. His book *Heaven and Hell* described his belief in a perfect spiritual body within the physical one. This idea matched Helen's belief that though her body was held back by its blindness and deafness, her soul was whole. She became a devoted follower of Swedenborg's teachings. Her own book *My Religion* was written partly to inspire more people to study Swedenborg's beliefs.

improved her speech as she had hoped. And it certainly couldn't prepare her for a school as challenging as Radcliffe. Radcliffe was Harvard's sister college and had the same high standards. Students studied the same subjects and took the same examinations.

Braillewriter

The Braillewriter, introduced in 1892 by Frank Haven Hall, was similar to a typewriter, except that there isn't a key for every letter. Since Braille letters are made of an arrangement of six dots, the machine has one key for each dot. Another part of the machine—an embosser—brings the keys together to produce the Braille letters.

The Cambridge School for Young Ladies, a school near Boston had been created specifically to prepare girls to attend Radcliffe. Annie and Helen decided it was the right place for Helen to begin.

Annie went to Cambridge, Massachusetts, to ask Arthur Gilman, director of the Cambridge School, for his permission for Helen Keller to study there. It was a surprising question to Gilman, whose school was attended by only hearing, sighted girls. But it was a challenge he couldn't resist.

With permission granted, Helen would need money to pay for the school. Again, Helen's generous and devoted friends stepped in to help. Eleanor Hutton, who with her husband Laurence counted many wealthy people among her friends, put together a fund. Others, including Dr. Bell, contributed enough money to ensure Helen's education was paid for. So, in October 1896, Helen began classes at the Cambridge School.

From the start, it was hard work. Helen was studying history, math, German, Latin, and literature, among other subjects. Arthur Gilman and Helen's German teacher learned the manual alphabet so they could talk to Helen. The other teachers didn't know how to communicate with Helen, so Annie would sit in class with Helen and spell the lessons into her hand. Helen couldn't take notes, but would go home and type the lessons from memory on a special typewriter called a Braillewriter. Since many of the books Helen was required to read were not available in Braille, Annie would also read those to her.

Throughout Helen's life, there were those who suspected that Annie was really the brilliant one—and that Helen was only repeating what her teacher told her. The Cambridge School, aware of these suspicions, went to great efforts to avoid any appearances of cheating or fraud. Annie was not allowed to be with Helen during examinations. Instead, Gilman spelled the questions into

Helen never sent out a typed letter that had any mistakes. She would retype it until it was completely free of errors.

Helen's hand. Helen then typed her answers on her special typewriter. These conditions made learning and studying even harder for Helen.

It was a good year for Helen, despite the hard work. Her younger sister, Mildred, with whom she had become quite close, had joined her at school in the middle of the year.

Helen passed all her exams, and Gilman reported that "No candidate in Harvard or Radcliffe was graded higher than Helen for English."

Everyone was so thrilled with Helen's progress that Annie and Gilman agreed that the standard five-year period to prepare for Radcliffe could be reduced to only three more.

But the second year proved far more difficult, both academically and personally. Mathematics made up the bulk of Helen's classes; her grades declined and her disappointment grew. Also, many of her textbooks were unavailable in Braille, so Annie had to read them, then interpret them to Helen. With Annie's own eyes growing more tired, it was painstaking work.

To add to the pressure, Annie, fearful that those supporting Helen's education would lose interest if it took Helen too long, pushed to speed her progress even more—

> *"The hilltop hour would not be half so wonderful if there were no dark valleys to traverse."*
>
> Helen Keller

reducing the time Helen had to finish
her coursework from three years to two.

Helen was feeling lonelier than ever.
Though the other girls were polite
with her, she felt very isolated
because of her disabilities. Few
knew the manual alphabet, so
she was unable to communicate
with other girls.

Helen was also maturing.
She better understood people's
temperaments and, in particular,
was more aware of Annie's
sometimes difficult nature. She was
accustomed to Annie's angry flare-
ups. But Annie also suffered

Annie worried about what
her role in Helen's life would
be as Helen grew older and
more independent.

occasional bouts of depression during which she would
disappear for hours. Helen was left feeling very alone.

Annie had very high expectations of Helen and
accepted nothing less than the best. Teachers at the school
reported that Annie accused Helen of making "stupid
remarks" and often became very impatient with Helen.
Though Helen was occasionally bewildered by Annie and
her moods, she remained almost entirely dependent upon
her. And, of course, she loved Annie like a mother.

Arthur Gilman was becoming concerned about the
relationship between Annie and Helen. He had spoken or

corresponded with a number of people who knew Helen and Annie, including Mr. Anagnos from Perkins. Many seemed concerned that Annie was pushing Helen too hard.

When Helen took to her bed for three days because of her menstrual period, which for her was quite painful, Gilman concluded that she was approaching a nervous breakdown from overwork. He decided the time had come to find someone else to teach Helen. He sent a number of letters to Kate Keller, hoping to persuade her that Annie was no longer good for Helen. He reported that Helen was overworked and exhausted. He also pointed out that Helen held a higher social standing than Annie, who had been born to poor Irish immigrant parents. Annie had taken great pains to conceal her early life from most

Helen and Annie used the finger alphabet to communicate almost as quickly as most people talk—about 80 words per minute.

people, knowing she'd be judged inferior. She had told Helen stories about her beloved brother and the fun they had. She'd never told Helen about Tewksbury. But even without knowing about that part of Annie's life, some people thought she was low-class because she was a child of immigrants. Arthur Gilman requested that Kate Keller appoint him as Helen's guardian. She finally agreed.

When Annie learned of this plot to separate Helen from her, her quick temper exploded. She told Gilman she was leaving the school with Helen and Mildred. He argued that she couldn't do that—she was no longer Helen's guardian.

When Annie told Helen what was happening, Helen was shattered. As she and Mildred clung together sobbing, Teacher left to visit friends in Boston.

Annie was frantic. What would her life be like without Helen? She could barely imagine it. Crossing the

> ## "My birthday can never mean as much to me as the arrival of Annie Sullivan on March 3, 1887. That was my soul's birthday."
>
> Helen Keller

river, she even considered drowning herself.

Instead, she gathered her wits and, on the advice of her friends, summoned Kate Keller. Annie also contacted Alexander Graham Bell, who sent his secretary John Hitz, a great friend to both Annie and Helen. And she contacted another friend—J.E. "Ed" Chamberlin, editor of *The Youth's Companion* and Helen's friend ever since he had published her story.

Helen was panicked. She refused to eat or sleep. To Helen, life without Teacher was unthinkable. Annie had her faults, Helen knew, but didn't everyone? And didn't she owe everything to her teacher? Annie had opened the world to her, lighting her darkness. The day she met Annie was more important than the day she was born—she called it her "soul's birthday."

Mildred was no better. She neither slept nor ate.

But Annie, armed with determination, returned to the school and demanded to see Helen and Mildred. Gilman gave in to Annie's demands only when she refused to leave. Chamberlin arrived later and took the two Keller girls and Annie with him to his home in Wrentham, Massachusetts. When Kate Keller arrived at the Chamberlin home, she found her daughters utterly distraught. She talked the situation over with the friends who had gathered and quickly changed her mind about firing Annie. She also sent a note to Arthur Gilman, informing him that her daughters were formally withdrawing from his school.

The crisis was over. Helen and Annie were overjoyed. Indeed, Helen had confessed to "Uncle Ed" that, if forced to choose between her teacher and her mother, she would choose her teacher. They would be together— for always, they believed.

Helen often defended Annie against those who disliked or mistrusted her. Helen attributed Annie's difficult personality to her high intelligence.

14

Writing Her Life

Helen and Annie didn't return to Cambridge. They decided to stay with the Chamberlins that winter and spring, and a tutor was found for Helen. In between cramming for the exams she was required to pass to enter Radcliffe, Helen managed to squeeze in some fun. She loved the Chamberlin family—and they her.

But the studying was grueling. Helen had to learn Greek, Latin, algebra, and geometry. While Greek and Latin came easily to Helen, math remained a constant struggle. Some friends suggested she abandon the subject—and the dean of Radcliffe agreed to let her substitute other courses—but Helen remained stubborn. To her, it was another challenge to overcome. And she did overcome it, passing her entrance exams and receiving her letter of admission to Radcliffe. Helen was ready.

It seemed, however, that Radcliffe wasn't ready for Helen. The dean of Radcliffe suggested that Helen take a year to focus on courses that were easy for her—writing, in Helen's case. Helen agreed, although halfheartedly. Annie was furious, convinced that Arthur Gilman was behind this plot to keep Helen out of Radcliffe. Helen had also been accepted to Cornell University and the University of Chicago, but she was determined to go to Radcliffe. She admitted later that the reason she insisted on Radcliffe was because "they didn't want me."

In May 1900, Helen

Helen's letter of acceptance to Radcliffe College arrived in 1899. Radcliffe's campus sits just outside of Boston, near its brother school, Harvard University.

wrote to Radcliffe and announced that she was ready for regular courses. It was a subtle way of pointing out that she had her letter of acceptance and now they must let her in.

The school officials agreed, but only with certain rules in place. Some critics had suggested that Annie would really be the one attending Radcliffe, and the school was determined to make it clear this would not be the case. The rules required that Annie leave the building the minute exams were being carried to the examination room. Two proctors would be hired to monitor Helen during each exam—one to monitor Helen, the other to monitor

Though she and Annie continued to enjoy each other's company, Helen felt isolated from the other students at Radcliffe.

Helen's proctor. A special typist would accompany Helen to immediately transcribed each exam into Braille for her. If Helen had any questions to ask, they would be answered by the Braille typist in the manual language. All communication must also be spoken aloud so the proctors could record it. Helen's records would be kept in the dean's office.

With the rules in place, the school was ready to make history by admitting 20-year-old Helen Keller, the first person with her handicaps to attend a university. She arrived in the fall of 1900.

Helen had looked forward to this day for years. But the Radcliffe years were, for the most part, disappointing for Helen. She found her course load staggering, leaving little time for other interests. She longed for the days when she could daydream and reflect about things. She was also aware of a social aspect of college that escaped her. She was the only deaf-blind girl, and her limitations as well as her fame no doubt made the other girls uncomfortable. They were kind enough—they even bought her a bulldog she named Phiz—but she would have preferred their friendship. Also, she and Annie lived off campus, which kept them apart from much of the activity.

Annie was reading and spelling to Helen for four or five hours a day. Her eyes were becoming more and more weak. Both she and Helen knew she was losing her sight, and both were terrified by the prospect of Annie becoming blind— Annie said that she'd rather kill herself. Helen knew about

Annie's dramatics, but still she tried hard to lessen Annie's workload. She only had Annie read things once, even though it would have helped her if Annie had repeated certain passages. But even this was too much. Annie's ophthalmologist—her eye doctor—insisted that she rest her eyes or she would, indeed, go blind.

John Albert Macy was hired to be Helen's editor, but he also became a valuable friend to both Helen and Annie.

Radcliffe did offer some bright spots for Helen. One was her English teacher, Dr. Charles Copeland. He believed that Helen's writing was among the best he had come across in his classes. But he wanted her to write more personally—more about her own unique world. At first, Helen was hurt by his criticism. Then she realized that he had pointed out exactly what she found missing in her own writing. She resolved to be herself, to write her own thoughts and own ideas. Helen was becoming independent.

As a result, her writing skills grew. Her talent was noticed by the editors of *Ladies' Home Journal.* They asked Helen to write the story of her life. It would be published in five monthly installments in the magazine. The fee they offered was three thousand dollars—a huge sum compared to the average salary at that time, which was less than $700 per year.

Since supporting themselves financially was an almost constant struggle for Helen and Annie, it was a tempting sum. With Annie's encouragement, Helen agreed. She felt pleased that she would be earning money on her own. But she soon found that writing the story and keeping up with school was an impossible task. Helen needed help. A friend introduced Helen and Annie to John Macy, a young English instructor at Harvard and an editor at *The Youth's Companion*. Helen liked him immediately. He quickly learned the manual alphabet to begin helping Helen edit her work. John Macy was convinced not only that could Helen write the magazine pieces, but that her work could also be expanded into a book—and he convinced Helen of this. He helped her negotiate a book contract, and in

Helen's autobiography was mostly well received, but she faced some criticism for describing things she hadn't seen or heard herself.

1903 *The Story of My Life*, by Helen Keller, was published by Doubleday, Page & Company.

John Macy was amazed by Helen. Her incredible memory astonished him, and he noted in his preface that she could recall long passages that she hadn't read in weeks. He was also impressed with her desire to constantly improve her writing. He was equally impressed with Helen's teacher and found himself falling in love with her. He even helped her silence the rumors that Annie was either the brains behind Helen Keller or else someone without talent of her own, with only eyes and fingers to help Helen.

The book was well received, if not the wild success that Helen and John Macy had hoped it would be. The publisher assured Helen and John that the book would live on. Indeed it has, becoming an international bestseller. It has been published in more than 50 languages and remains in print 100 years later. In June 1904, on the day

Helen graduated from Radcliffe with honors. She was now the most well-educated deaf-blind person in the world.

after her twenty-fourth
birthday, Helen stood in
cap and gown to receive
her diploma from
Radcliffe. Beside Helen

BACHELOR OF ARTS

A bachelor of arts degree is awarded to someone who has completed a required college course of study.

was, of course, Annie Sullivan. When Helen's name was
called, the two women walked gracefully across the stage,
where Helen received her diploma. It noted that she had
achieved a bachelor of arts degree with the added
distinction: *cum laude*—"with praise."

Helen felt satisfied with her achievement, as did Annie
(though she had hoped Helen would graduate *summa cum
laude*—the highest honor). But Helen was angry that
Radcliffe didn't acknowledge the large role that Annie played
in helping Helen graduate. Even years later, it stung Helen
that Annie was overlooked. But, for the moment, Helen
relished her accomplishment.

A small group of friends joined Helen to celebrate her day.
Her mother was unable to attend, but the devoted John Hitz,
Bell's secretary, was there. Also there was John Macy.

Though Annie had fallen in love with John, she was torn
between wanting to marry him and wanting to stay at
Helen's side. She also worried about the age difference
between them—she was 11 years older. For more than a
year, she wavered between saying yes to John's marriage
proposal and saying no. But when John told Helen about
the proposal, she told both of them to go ahead. They

reassured her that she would always be with them. Finally, in a small ceremony at Annie and Helen's home in Wrentham, Annie and John Macy were married.

Marriage was a dream Helen also wanted for herself. At 24, Helen was a lovely woman with a beautiful figure. But though she was interested in men, she felt conflicted about love and marriage. She wondered who would want to be burdened with someone like her. "I can't imagine a man

Helen, Annie, and John lived in a rambling farmhouse in Wrentham, Massachusetts.

> ## "I should think it would seem like marrying a statue."
>
> Helen Keller

wanting to marry me," she once said to Alexander Graham Bell. "I should think it would seem like marrying a statue." For years, it hadn't mattered. Between Kate Keller and Annie, no man had managed to get close enough to Helen to become a suitor.

The trio of John, Annie, and Helen lived happily together in their farmhouse in Wrentham. It felt like home to Helen, who knew every corner of every room. She happily contributed to the running of the household by washing dishes, clearing the table, and making beds. They often entertained friends, each of whom Helen welcomed and recognized with a simple grasp of a hand.

John brought joy to both Annie and Helen. He was Helen's editor and most severe critic, but he also brought her work up to a standard that pleased her. He built a system of wire and ropes so that Helen could walk safely outside by herself and enjoy the garden. Together she and John would cycle on the sociable bike—the faster, the better for Helen. At night, Annie, John, Helen—and friends if they were there—would discuss religion, politics, and more into the night. They often disagreed, but allowed each other their differences of opinion.

It was through her conversations with John Macy that Helen developed the ideas about society that would alter the course of her life.

chapter 15

Socialism and the Stage

John Macy was a socialist. Helen loved to listen to him discuss his ideals, which, partly at least, matched her own. It was a time in America when socialism was gaining popularity. To Helen, socialism was about equality, peace, and education for all. Her friends insisted that Helen's "politics" had always been there. They pointed to her instinctive urge to champion the cause of anyone in need of help: the poor, the oppressed, the uneducated.

It was during this time that Helen discovered what would become her life's work: campaigning on behalf of the blind. She learned that most blindness was the result of poverty—poor living conditions, lack of nutrition, no access to proper medical care. And there were few schools for blind children and little training or jobs for blind adults.

After graduating, Helen devoted much of her time to writing about social problems, such as poverty and services for the blind.

In 1907, Helen wrote an article for *Ladies' Home Journal* that talked about ophthalmia neonatorum, an

CAPITALISM/SOCIALISM

Capitalism is an economic system based on private ownership of wealth and businesses. Socialism is based on shared ownership of the wealth an economy produces.

infection that mothers with syphilis, a sexually transmitted disease, passed to their infants, causing blindness. Preventing the infection was simple and cheap—it required putting a solution of silver nitrate into the eyes of newborn children. But treatment wasn't required by American law, and it was not commonly offered. It was a courageous article for Helen to write; in those days, young women never spoke about sexually transmitted disease, let alone wrote about it. But Helen was outraged. She felt that mothers needed to demand this treatment for their babies. Blindness caused by this lack of treatment could be—and should be—wiped out.

Then, in 1909, Helen became a member of the Socialist Party. It was a daring move, and one she concealed for a time. Her living expenses were funded by wealthy capitalists, who were opposed to socialism. Helen's and Annie's money was dwindling. But when multimillionaire Andrew Carnegie offered Helen five thousand dollars a year through a plan that supported outstanding Americans, Helen declined. Though money was scarce, she felt she couldn't take money from a famous capitalist. Carnegie was noted for making his fortune from producing steel, and he profited from the labor of his workers. He was, quite possibly, the world's richest man. By this time he had sold his steel company and wanted to share his wealth to support education and libraries, but Helen still objected to taking his money.

Helen sympathized with workers—including women and children—who suffered awful working conditions and had little power to change them. Rather than feeling alone as she had most of her life, Helen felt that she shared a common plight

The suffragists believed in and fought for women's right to vote. They often held demonstrations and rallies to gain support.

with these people. She was furious at how the country's least powerful people were being treated. Helen began to express this anger freely, revealing to the world her membership in a socialist group and writing articles and letters expressing her beliefs.

In 1913, she published *Out of the Dark*, a collection of essays in which she examined her socialist views and explained them to readers. The book flopped. People didn't want to read about Helen's politics. Most wanted her to be—or at least appear to be—the saintlike handicapped woman who accepted her fate with a gentle smile on her face.

Helen was partly to blame for that image. She knew that many people expected this of her, and she had obliged for much of her life. But she was also a highly intelligent, passionate, and determined woman.

Couldn't people accept her as a whole person?

Many could not. As Helen continued to fight openly for her causes, she suffered criticism and even disdain. She couldn't possibly know politics, some newspapers claimed, because of her handicaps. Clearly, they proposed, she was being used by socialists to advance their own views. These remarks stung Helen, but she didn't back down. She continued to work for the causes she believed in. She was active in the suffrage movement, which stood for equal rights, including voting rights, for women. She also fought for fair pay and job security for workers. She bore the criticism against her as well as she could.

Things were no better at home. Annie was depressed and tired. John had left for a job in New York, and Annie and Helen didn't want to join him. Money was tighter than ever. To earn an income, Helen wanted to embark on a lecture tour. She was even taking voice lessons in hopes of improving her speech.

When Annie suddenly required surgery, John returned home to be with her. Helen suspected the marriage was in trouble but was glad to have John back home. He helped her prepare for her lecture tour, choosing where it would take place and how much to charge for the tickets. He even helped write the speeches.

In February 1913, Helen was ready to take to the stage, with Annie at her side. She was terrified. She described it by saying: "My mind froze, my heart stopped beating....Until my dying day I shall think of that stage as a pillory where I stood cold, riveted, trembling, voiceless."

But though her voice was sometimes hard to understand, it served her well—that day and on many others. She and

Annie developed a routine. Annie would speak for about an hour, telling the audience about how she first met Helen and taught the young girl. Then Helen would be brought out to the platform. She would place her fingers on Annie's mouth to illustrate lipreading. Then she would talk, offering her own brand of inspiration and advice.

At the end, the audience was invited to ask questions. Most were expected, and Helen endured them with trademark good humor: "How do you tell day from night?" "Can you tell colors apart?" And, always, "Do you close your eyes when you're asleep?"

"I don't know," she would always reply to this last question. "I never stayed awake to find out."

Helen and Annie toured for a few months, until one day Annie became so ill she couldn't continue. They returned home.

The First Appearance on the Lecture Platform of

HELEN KELLER

And her Teacher Mrs. Macy (Anne M. Sullivan)

SUBJECT
"The Heart and the Hand," or the Right Use of our Senses

Under the exclusive Management of
J. B. POND LYCEUM BUREAU
Metropolitan Life Building
New York City

A flyer advertises Helen and Annie's lectures, which attracted many people who were curious about how Helen communicated.

Polly Thomson (top right) was hired to help Annie work with Helen, but Annie and Helen remained as close as ever.

Frightened at the prospect of having no money coming in, Helen gave in and accepted Andrew Carnegie's offer. He was delighted, and sent the first of the checks that would continue for the rest of Helen's life.

Annie recovered, and in January 1914, the two women prepared for the lecture circuit again, this time accompanied by Helen's mother. They would cover the continent—speaking everywhere from large halls in cities to tents set up in the country.

In the meantime, Annie and John's marriage was falling apart. And the United States was preparing to enter the First World War. Helen was opposed to both. She wanted Annie and John to work out their differences. And she wanted her country to stay out of war. She wouldn't get either wish.

Helen set out again on a lecture tour in 1915. This time she and Annie were accompanied by Polly Thomson, a new secretary who had been hired to take some of the workload and stress off of Annie.

The lectures were a huge success. Helen had become one of the most famous women in the world. Audiences that included Thomas Edison and Henry Ford crowded into auditoriums to hear her speak.

The summer of 1916 was a difficult one for Helen. After returning from yet another lecture tour, Annie was diagnosed with tuberculosis—the same disease that had killed her mother and her brother, Jimmie. Annie was convinced that she needed to go to a rest home in Lake Placid, New York, to recover. It was decided that when Annie left, Helen would go to Alabama with her mother. Even Polly was gone on vacation in Scotland. A new secretary, Peter Fagan, was helping out in Polly's absence.

Though Annie hadn't yet left for Lake Placid, she had taken to her bed. Helen felt overwhelmed, depressed, and utterly alone when Peter approached her. She was shocked when he took her hand tenderly and confessed his feelings for her. He even told her he hoped to marry her—and was prepared for all that would mean. "His love was a bright sun that shone upon my helplessness and isolation," Helen later wrote.

Helen was delighted. Peter's advances were sudden, but certainly not unwelcome. He convinced Helen not to tell anyone—not yet. So the two took walks together in the woods, enjoyed books together, and fell deeply in love.

16

Helen's Life Work

Helen longed to tell Annie and her mother about Peter. Peter had even applied for a license to marry Helen. But before Helen could reveal her secret romance, her mother read a newspaper article that mentioned the marriage license application. Kate Keller was furious. Peter Fagan was not good enough for her daughter—perhaps no man ever could be. She threw him out of the house and immediately took Helen to Mildred's home in Alabama.

But Peter was determined and resourceful. He managed to get letters typed in Braille to Helen. He planned to elope. One night, Helen managed to pack a bag and sneak out to the porch. In the morning, Mildred found her waiting, suitcase at her side. She had waited all night, but Peter never showed up. With her disabilities, Helen had no way to find out what happened.

Helen was very disappointed, but came to believe that it was for the best. Nonetheless, she

Helen was in her late 30s when she fell in love. She called that time her "little island of joy."

referred to the time when love had entered her life as her "little island of joy."

Helen missed Annie terribly. Their financial affairs were a mess, and Helen had no idea how to manage them. Then, in 1917, the United States entered World War I. Suddenly Helen's socialist views were not only daring, they were considered dangerous. The government clamped down on anyone and anything that didn't agree with its own pro-war stand. The war also drove up the cost of living.

World War I

World War I broke out in June 1914. The United States was determined to stay neutral. Then, on May 7, 1915, a German submarine sank the British ocean liner *Lusitania*. More than 1,200 people were killed, including many Americans. In 1917, the United States entered the war.

Annie had returned home, but she and Helen found it too expensive to keep up their house in Wrentham. They decided to sell it, and moved to a red brick cottage in Forest Hills, New York. The good news was that Annie's diagnosis of tuberculosis turned out to be wrong. She wasn't dying, after all.

Early the following year, 1918, Hollywood came knocking at Helen's door. Moving pictures, or movies, were becoming very popular. Lured by the promise of a large paycheck and the chance to tell the world her story, Helen agreed to help make a movie about her incredible life.

Then, at the same time the producer was getting ready to start filming, Helen was invited to make a speech. In it, she spoke in support of the Industrial Workers of the World, or Wobblies as they were called. Helen supported this union and its radical ideas. She spoke out against the government's persecution of them. It was a bold speech to give, especially during wartime.

The film's producer panicked. He feared that Helen's opinions would ruin the film's chances for success. Theaters could refuse to play the film, and the public could refuse to see it. Helen agreed to keep her anti-government opinions to herself. Shortly afterward, she and Annie headed out to California to help with the film.

Deliverance was a silent film—the technology to

WOMANHOOD—Helen Keller of today, with Mrs. Anne Sullivan Macy, for thirty years her teacher and friend (at right) and Miss Polly Thomson, her secretary (at left).

HELEN KELLER
IN
"DELIVERANCE"
"My Message to the World"

An Epoch-Making Three-Act Photo-Drama
By FRANCIS TREVELYAN MILLER

Produced and Directed by GEORGE FOSTER PLATT

GEORGE KLEINE
Motion Pictures

The movie **Deliverance**, about Helen's life, also featured her mother Kate and younger brother Phillips.

combine sound with movies had not yet been invented. Helen wanted it to show her life in an accurate and honest way. The film's producer and writers wanted suspense and drama. In the end, the film wasn't what Helen wanted, though it received good reviews. However, few people saw it, and it never made the money Helen and Annie had hoped for.

Still, the taste of success lingered, and Helen decided to create a vaudeville act. Vaudeville was bigger than films at the time—it was the country's most popular form of entertainment. Many people were surprised that Helen chose to do this; vaudeville was often considered vulgar. Along with the singers, dancers, acrobats, and comedians, some of the more notable vaudeville acts at the time included a woman who stripped naked to promote her antiaging remedies; the Human Tank, who swallowed frogs whole and threw them back up alive; and Professor Backwards, who could write upside-down and backward. Helen's friends tried to talk her out of doing vaudeville, but she needed the money. Besides, she liked being in the public eye. Annie was less enthusiastic, but she agreed.

A 20-minute act was created based on the lectures the pair had given a few years earlier. It opened on February 24, 1920, at the Palace Theater in New York. The show was such a success that it ran longer than originally planned. Helen and Annie traveled to other places where the show was also well received. Helen loved the life of vaudeville; she found the other performers interesting and colorful. Annie hated it. She thought the other performers were rude and crude. And Annie seemed to be frequently ill. She looked and felt exhausted. Still, it was making them money, and they needed money to live.

In Los Angeles one night in November 1921, Helen received word that her mother had died. Two hours later, she walked onstage and delivered a wonderful performance. She could indulge in her sorrow after the show, she had told herself. And that's what she did. But she was comforted, as always when she faced loss, by her spiritual faith.

Soon after Helen and Annie returned home to Forest Hills, Helen learned that her lifelong friend Dr. Alexander Graham Bell had died. It

Helen found performing fun and exciting. Annie found it exhausting and difficult. But both needed the money it earned them.

was another difficult loss, but again, Helen found comfort in the idea that she would meet him in heaven.

In the meantime, though, Helen needed to search for another career. She and Annie were done with vaudeville—and vaudeville with them. Annie had become too ill, too many times, and her eyesight was getting worse and worse. Besides, Helen and Annie had told their story all over the country. Without a way to create fresh material, they had no way to

Helen loved the glitzy costumes and excitement of vaudeville. She even learned to apply her own makeup.

keep audiences interested in coming back. Annie was glad it was over. Helen was worried. As usual, she needed to make a living. Annie now needed her, and Helen felt she owed it to Teacher, for all her years of devotion, to take care of her financially. And both she and Annie loved to splurge. When they had money, they spent it. And when they didn't, they needed to figure out a way to earn it.

Opportunity presented itself late in 1923. Helen had gathered friends together for Christmas Eve. One of those friends was Robert Irwin, the blind research director of the newly created American Foundation for the Blind (AFB). The AFB worked to help other agencies that worked for the blind. It undertook national and international projects such as developing a single Braille code to be used nationwide, increasing the number of books available in Braille, and finding jobs for the blind. Robert Irwin wanted Helen and Annie to become fundraisers.

Neither Helen nor Annie wanted to do this. However, Helen admired Robert Irwin and was impressed at what he'd accomplished so far. She and Annie agreed to a six-month trial period. After that, they'd decide whether to continue.

Together the two women again made the rounds, making speeches in which they talked about Helen's education and then asking for donations on behalf of the AFB. At first, they were only moderately successful. But then Helen began addressing politicians and lawmakers who promised to assist the AFB. The AFB was thrilled. Helen's name clearly had power.

Helen, with her companion Polly Thomson, became a powerful speaker on behalf of the American Foundation for the Blind.

In 1926, she charmed President Coolidge at the White House. Helen was doing more to raise public understanding and awareness about blindness than anyone before.

But in 1927, Helen took some time away from AFB to write another autobiography—this time covering the years following the publication of *The Story of My Life*. She was also

Helen managed to charm even President Calvin Coolidge, who had a reputation for being serious and stern.

approached to write about her religious beliefs and the teachings of Emanuel Swedenborg. Helen took on both projects, publishing *My Religion* that year. *Midstream: My Later Life* took much longer, and even with Annie's help—and the help of an editor named Nella Braddy Henney—it was a difficult process. *Midstream* was finally published in 1929. Helen was exhausted by the experience of writing it.

Annie and Nella

When Doubleday sent editor Nella Braddy Henney to help Helen with her book *Midstream*, no one dreamed she would end up writing a biography of Annie Sullivan. But Annie and Nella quickly became friends, and Annie began to confide in Nella. Nella believed that Annie's story was every bit as interesting as Helen's. Her biography of Annie was published in 1933.

chapter 17

Good-Bye to Teacher

The year 1929 was notable for other reasons: the crash of the stock market and the start of the Great Depression. It was also the year that doctors removed Annie's right eye to relieve some of her pain. Her left eye required surgery, too, but Annie's doctor recommended waiting as long as possible, as the operation could cause total blindness.

Annie was more depressed than ever, and Helen could feel that Annie's energy and enthusiasm were gone. Helen tried to convince her to take a trip to Paris to raise her spirits, but Annie refused.

Instead, Polly accompanied Helen on another trip to Washington, D.C., where Helen convinced Congress to support Braille books for the blind. Congress agreed to designate $75,000 to the cause. It wasn't a lot of money, but it was a huge victory for Helen: This was the first time that the United States government had ever funded

Annie (right) had been Helen's companion for more than four decades, but she was becoming tired and was frequently ill.

programs for the blind.

Then Annie changed her mind about traveling, and in 1930 the three women— Annie, Polly, and Helen— set off for a six-month visit to Ireland, England, and Scotland, where Polly had family. Helen hoped that the trip would help Annie feel better. But Annie was only becoming more frail and frustrated. Helen, who celebrated her fiftieth birthday during the trip, was still strong and healthy.

The Great Depression

On October 24, 1929, a day that became known as Black Thursday, stock prices crashed at the New York Stock Exchange. Millions of dollars were lost, and a period of worldwide economic troubles known as the Great Depression began. Many people lost their life savings. Many formerly wealthy people suddenly found themselves with nothing and struggled to pay for food and other necessities.

In the spring of 1931, Helen played a key role for the American Foundation for the Blind as it hosted the first international conference of workers for the blind. The event was held in New York, and workers from 32 countries attended. Helen raised funds, delivered speeches, held a reception, and even presented the delegates to the president and first lady of the United States. Helen thrived on the excitement and the feeling that she was doing so much for the millions of blind people around the world.

A couple of months later, Helen received an invitation from the government of Yugoslavia. The kingdom invited Helen and her two companions to visit and discuss how best to help the blind. It was the start of Helen's international work as a spokesperson for the AFB. Many other invitations followed, and in each foreign country, Helen Keller was treated royally. She enjoyed being a role model for the blind.

Annie admitted that she wasn't being the least bit courageous or positive about losing her sight, though she had always tried to encourage others. Her health was also getting worse. It was

Polly Thomson stepped in to take Annie's place on Helen's trips, including many to foreign countries.

time to consider what Helen would do after Annie was gone. Though Helen hated the thought of life without Teacher, she knew she needed someone to take care of her affairs. She couldn't stand concerning herself with money. She just wanted to do what she did best: help the blind.

The AFB's president, M.C. Migel, agreed. He felt strongly that Helen Keller had done more to help the cause than anyone, and that the foundation owed it to her to ensure she was cared for the rest of her life. He promised that the foundation—with a committee chosen by Helen to manage her money and affairs—would provide for Helen. Helen could relax. Her future was in trustworthy hands.

More good news came when Franklin Delano Roosevelt won the 1932 presidential election. Helen liked FDR—she felt sure that the country was being run by a good man. FDR also admired Helen. He had his own physical disability (polio had paralyzed his legs in 1921) which he tried to downplay to the public. But Helen knew he dealt daily with his handicap and felt a kinship toward him.

Helen, Annie, and Polly spent the summer of 1932 vacationing in England and Scotland. As they arrived at the farmhouse they had rented in South Arcan, Scotland, Annie received a telegram. John Macy, her husband, was dead.

Annie was devastated. Though they hadn't lived together for years, she still felt a great deal of affection for John, and his death was hard to accept.

A year later, a biography of Annie, written by Nella Braddy Henney, who had worked with Helen on *Midstream*, was published. Annie, however, was slowly dying, and seemed to barely acknowledge the book. Helen was as strong and determined as ever, and her influence continued to grow. She pushed the government further for more

Helen visited Paris to honor the hundredth anniversary of the death of Louis Braille.

assistance to the blind. In 1935, President Roosevent signed the Social Security Act, which offered unemployment insurance, retirement funds, and assistance for children and the disabled. Thanks to Helen's hard work, the blind were included in the category of "disabled," which meant they could apply for financial help.

First Lady Eleanor Roosevelt was a fan of Helen's and noted, "Miss Keller and my husband typified the triumph over physical handicap."

Almost a year later, in the summer of 1936, Annie drifted into a coma. She died a few months later, on October 20, 1936, with Helen at her side, holding her hand.

Helen had lost the person who meant the most to her. Annie had been, in so many ways, Helen's link to the seeing-hearing world. Her friends feared that Helen would fall apart. But Helen held herself together through the following days, including Teacher's funeral at Marble Collegiate Church in New York. Annie's remains were placed in the National Cathedral in Washington. It was the first time a woman had received such an honor.

After the funeral, Helen and Polly went back to Scotland, where Helen hoped to find some comfort. At first, she felt dazed and barely ate or slept. But as always, her faith lifted her up and urged her on. Life slowly returned to normal.

Helen received an invitation from a publisher who wanted to print her journal, which she had continued to keep up through the years. The publisher encouraged her to simply submit her day-to-day notes. Helen was intrigued. She believed it would be a chance for the world to see that she could indeed stand on her own two feet, thanks to all that Annie had done for her.

Helen received another invitation, this time from a blind writer in Japan who wanted Helen to visit his country. Helen accepted.

The National Cathedral in Washington, D.C. holds the remains of many famous Americans including Annie, Helen, and Polly.

Preparations for the trip to Japan were extensive. Helen would be delivering dozens of speeches throughout her stay. She would be meeting hundreds of people. She bought herself new clothes and spent hours working on her speeches. She was acutely aware of Annie's absence but threw herself into getting ready for the trip. Even President Roosevelt sent Helen off with a message to the people of Japan, noting that Helen would undoubtedly inspire them. He knew she continued to inspire countless Americans.

The trip was a wonderful success. Everywhere Helen and Polly went, they

Helen and Polly had a very successful visit to Japan, where they were treated to a taste of Japanese culture.

were greeted enthusiastically. They were welcomed by princes and politicians, even the emperor. It was exhausting but very satisfying work.

When Helen returned home, her *Journal* was published. Anyone who had doubts about whether Helen could survive without Teacher had to admit that she seemed to be coping well. In spite of the huge loss that Helen had suffered when Annie died, she seemed to be doing fine.

In 1938, Helen and Polly

Pearl Harbor

The United States had remained neutral during the early months of World War II. Then, on December 7, 1941, in a surprise attack, the Japanese bombed the American fleet on Pearl Harbor in Hawaii. 2,433 were killed, 1,178 wounded, 18 warships sunk, and 188 planes destroyed. The United States was in the war.

moved into Arcan Ridge, a home that had been built for them in Westport, Connecticut, with help from friends and the AFB. It was named after the special place Helen, Polly, and Annie had visited in Scotland.

The following year, war broke out in Europe. Two years later, Japan bombed Pearl Harbor, bringing the United States into World War II. Helen was devastated—the friendship she had felt for the Japanese after her visit was gone.

But the war also took Helen to her next life stage.

chapter 18

A Life Well Lived

World War II created thousands of war veterans who needed Helen's particular brand of optimism and courage. Helen wanted to help, and she asked the foundation's assistance in arranging visits to wounded men. Helen clearly knew in her heart how the wounded men felt: Life wasn't over, she told them. It was different but not over. And they could still find meaning and satisfaction in it. It was a message she lived herself. But Helen herself gained enormously from her visits. She

Helen helped wounded war veterans deal realistically with their disabilities. She represented the ability to triumph.

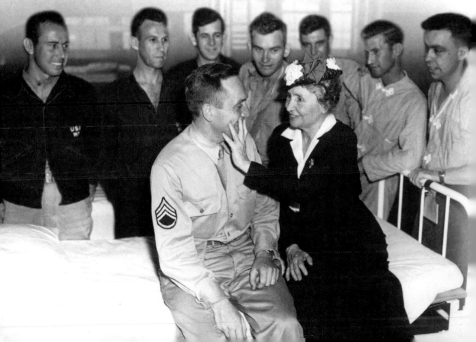

called them "the crowning experience of my life."

In 1946, Helen started out on her first world tour for the AFB. Over the next 11 years, she would visit 35 countries. As her influence grew, she was instrumental in changing circumstances for the blind and deaf-blind around the world.

In November of 1946, while Helen and Polly were in Rome, they received word that Arcan Ridge, their beloved Connecticut home had burned down. They lost everything, including all of Helen's and Annie's letters, as well as 20 years' worth of notes for a book Helen was planning to write about

An Oscar for Helen

The documentary *Helen Keller in Her Story* won the Oscar for best feature-length documentary film at the 1955 Academy Awards. It was originally released as *The Unconquered* and was produced by Nancy Hamilton, a friend of Helen's. Helen was pleased with the film, though at least one close friend believed it didn't give a realistic portrayal of Helen's life or the extent of her disabilities.

Annie. Helen took the tragedy in stride, noting that the horror and devastation she witnessed in Europe—the aftermath of the war—was worse than anything she had endured.

Helen's life was captured on film through a documentary released in 1954. It featured Helen herself and was titled *The*

Unconquered (later
released as *Helen Keller
in Her Story*) and won
an Academy Award. That
same year, she resumed work
on her book about Teacher. It was tough to dredge up
painful memories, but Helen enjoyed writing it more than
any of her other books.

In 1959, *The Miracle Worker* was presented on Broadway
to rave reviews. William Gibson's play tells the story of
young Helen when Annie Sullivan first arrived. A movie
based on the play earned Academy Awards for the actors
who played Annie and Helen.

Two years after the opening of *The Miracle Worker*, Helen
suffered the first of a number of small strokes, which occur
when the blood supply to the brain is blocked. Each stroke
left her abilities slightly more impaired. Helen also developed
diabetes, which made it more difficult for her to travel or
even walk. For the next seven years, she was confined to a
wheelchair and bed. Her work with the AFB was over, and
she spent her days reading her beloved books and devoting
her life to "study" as she had said she would. She still met her
friends, and many claimed Helen seemed to be having fun

for the first time in her life. Perhaps it was the first time she was able to simply enjoy her life, without attempting to prove anything to the world.

In 1964, President Lyndon Johnson awarded Helen the Presidential Medal of Freedom, the nation's highest civilian award. A year later, she was elected to the Women's Hall of Fame at the New York World's Fair.

The Presidential Medal of Freedom, a wartime medal, was reintroduced in 1963 as an honor for distinguished civilian service in peacetime.

Helen had a heart attack in late May of 1968. A few days later, on June 1, Helen Keller died quietly, according to the nurse who was with her. Death was something Helen had not feared; she was sure that, in the next stage, she would be able both to see and hear. In the end, she died as she had lived: dignified and courageous, with her sightless eyes focused firmly on the future.

Patty Duke, who played young Helen in *The Miracle Worker*, was delighted and surprised that the real Helen was so much fun.

Events in the Life of Helen Keller

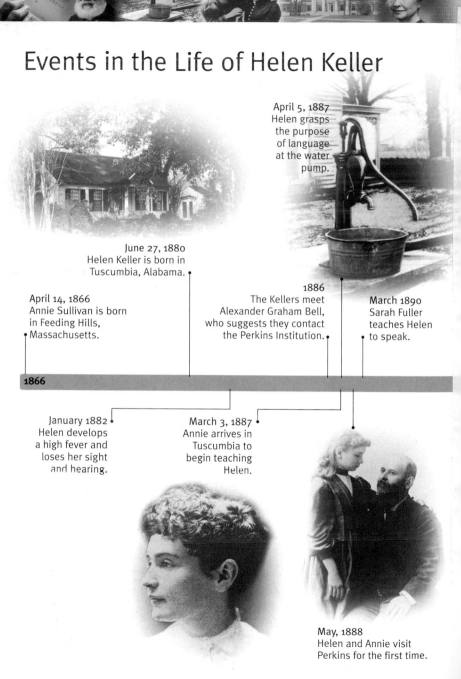

April 5, 1887
Helen grasps the purpose of language at the water pump.

June 27, 1880
Helen Keller is born in Tuscumbia, Alabama.

April 14, 1866
Annie Sullivan is born in Feeding Hills, Massachusetts.

1886
The Kellers meet Alexander Graham Bell, who suggests they contact the Perkins Institution.

March 1890
Sarah Fuller teaches Helen to speak.

1866

January 1882
Helen develops a high fever and loses her sight and hearing.

March 3, 1887
Annie arrives in Tuscumbia to begin teaching Helen.

May, 1888
Helen and Annie visit Perkins for the first time.

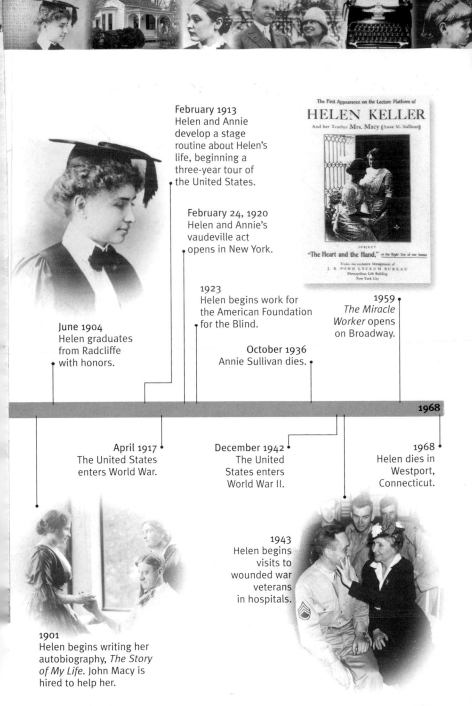

February 1913
Helen and Annie develop a stage routine about Helen's life, beginning a three-year tour of the United States.

February 24, 1920
Helen and Annie's vaudeville act opens in New York.

The First Appearance on the Lecture Platform of
HELEN KELLER
And her Teacher Mrs. Macy (Anne M. Sullivan)

"The Heart and the Hand," or the Right Use of our Senses

Under the exclusive Management of
J. B. POND LYCEUM BUREAU
Metropolitan Life Building
New York City

1923
Helen begins work for the American Foundation for the Blind.

1959
The Miracle Worker opens on Broadway.

June 1904
Helen graduates from Radcliffe with honors.

October 1936
Annie Sullivan dies.

1968

April 1917
The United States enters World War.

December 1942
The United States enters World War II.

1968
Helen dies in Westport, Connecticut.

1943
Helen begins visits to wounded war veterans in hospitals.

1901
Helen begins writing her autobiography, The Story of My Life. John Macy is hired to help her.

Bibliography

Books:

Dash, Joan. *World at Her Fingertips: The Story of Helen Keller.* New York: Scholastic, 2002.

Davidson, Margaret. *Helen Keller.* New York: Scholastic, 1989.

Davidson, Margaret. *Helen Keller's Teacher.* New York: Scholastic, 1992.

Helen Keller in Her Story. Dir. Nancy Hamilton. Albert Margolies, 1954.

Herrmann, Dorothy. *Helen Keller: A Life.* Chicago: Chicago UP, 1999.

Jennings, Peter and Todd Brewster. *The Century for Young People.* New York: Random House, 1999.

Keller, Helen. *My Religion.* Westchester: Swedenborg Foundation, 1960.

Keller, Helen. *The Story of My Life.* 100th Anniversary ed. New York: Signet, 2002.

Keller, Helen. *Teacher: Annie Sullivan Macy.* Westport, Connecticut: Greenwood Publishing Group, Incorporated, 1985.

Kudlinski, Kathleen V. *Helen Keller: A Light for the Blind.* New York: Viking Penguin, 1989.

Lawlor, Laurie. *Helen Keller, Rebellious Spirit: The Life and Times of Helen Keller.* New York: Holiday House, 2001.

MacLeod, Elizabeth. *Helen Keller: A Determined Life.* Tonawanda, New York: Kids Can Press, 2004.

The Miracle Worker. William Gibson, Screenwriter. Arthur Penn, director. United Artists, 1962.

St. George, Judith. *Dear Dr. Bell...Your friend, Helen Keller.* New York: G.P. Putnam's Sons, 1992.

Works Cited:

Page 11: "Come right away" *The Miracle Worker;* also *Helen Keller's Teacher,* p. 83.

Page 26: "Where's Helen?" *Helen Keller's Teacher,* p. 91.

Page 27: "You were brought here..." ibid, p. 93; also *The Miracle Worker.*

Page 36: "I never saw such..." *Helen Keller: A Life,* p. 43.

Page 37: "the wild creature..." ibid, p. 44.

Page 40: "for the first time..." *The Story of My Life,* p. 17.

Page 44: "life tumbled upon..." *Helen Keller: A Life,* p. 53; cited from *Teacher: Annie Sullivan Macy.*

Page 44: "Something tells me..." *Helen Keller: A Life;* cited from a letter from Annie to Sophia Hopkins.

Page 45: "hardly walk without stumbling..." *The Story of My Life,* p. 30.

Page 45: "I thank God..." *Helen Keller: A Life,* p. 61; cited from a letter from Annie Sullivan to Michael Anagnos.

Page 47: "The beautiful truth..." *The Story of My Life,* p. 22.

Page 47: "No barrier of the senses..." ibid, p. 89.

Page 50: "learned from life itself" ibid, p. 28.

Page 53: "phenomenon"; *Helen Keller: A Life,* p. 63; cited from the Perkins Institution Sixth Annual Report, written by Michael Anagnos.

Page 53: "What joy..." *The Story of My Life,* p. 32.

Page 54: "moved to tears"; *Helen Keller: A Life,* p. 72.

Page 54: "Who put salt in…" *The Story of My Life*, p. 35.
Page 57: "Sometimes I stood between…" ibid, p. 6.
Page 58: "It is too warm." ibid, p. 44.
Page 58: "I am not dumb now." ibid, p. 45.
Page 58: "I labored night and day…" ibid, p. 44.
Page 61: "plagiarism and deliberate falsehood" *Helen Keller: A Life*, p. 82.
Page 62: "I have ever since…" *The Story of My Life*, p. 50.
Page 63: "with a mind made clearer…" ibid, p. 55.
Page 67: "love or religion or goodness"; "everything" ibid, p. 55.
Page 69: "In the three weeks…" ibid, p. 57.
Page 69: "an author, to recognize…" ibid, p. 58.
Page 72: "The building is magnificent…" ibid, letter to Miss Caroline Derby, p. 182.
Page 73: "Not Harvard, Helen…" *Helen Keller*, p. 78; also *Helen Keller's Teacher*, p. 151.
Page 74: "My own dear loving…" *The Story of My Life*, letter to Charles Dudley Warner, p. 190.
Page 74: "death is no more than…" *Helen Keller: A Life*, p. 297.
Page 78: "no candidate in Harvard…" ibid, p. 116.
Page 85: "they didn't want me…" *World at her Fingertips*, Joan Dash (Scholastic, 2001), p. 94
Page 92: "I can't imagine a man…" *Helen Keller: A Life*, p. 129.
Page 98: "…my mind froze…" *World at Her Fingertips*, p. 136.
Page 99: "I don't know…" *Helen Keller: A Light for the Blind*, p. 38; also *Helen Keller*, p. 05.
Page 101: "His love was a bright sun…" *Dear Dr. Bell…Your friend, Helen Keller*, p. 76.
Page 103: "little island of joy…" *Helen Keller: A Life*, p. 198.
Page 118: "the crowning experience of…" ibid, p. 289.
Page 121: "gently…" ibid, p. 334.

For Further Study Visit

Helen Keller's work for the **American Foundation for the Blind (AFB)** (www.afb.org) spanned 44 years. A special collection recalls the many speeches and letters she wrote on the AFB's behalf, and includes photographs from Helen's life.

The **Perkins School for the Blind** (www.perkins.org) in Watertown, Massachusetts, honors its most famous alumnae with an exhibition on Helen Keller, Annie Sullivan, and Laura Bridgman in its museum. Tours of the school are another way to get a glimpse into Helen's life experience.

Helen Keller, Annie Sullivan, and Polly Thomson all received the high honor of burial at the **Washington National Cathedral** in Washington, D.C. (www.cathedral.org/cathedral/index.shtml). Tourists can visit the three tombs, which sit side-by-side in St. Joseph's Chapel.

Index

Picture Credits